The Record-breaking
SUNIL GAVASKAR

The Record-breaking
SUNIL GAVASKAR

C.D. CLARK

DAVID & CHARLES
Newton Abbot   London   North Pomfret (Vt)

British Library Cataloguing in Publication Data

Clark, C. D.
The record-breaking Sunil Gavaskar.
1. Gavaskar, Sunil
.2. Cricket players – India – Biography
I. Title
796.358'092'4   GV915.G38

ISBN 0–7153–8001–X

Library of Congress Catalog Card Number: 80-66423

© C. D. Clark   1980

All rights reserved. No part of this publication may be
reproduced, stored in a retrieval system, or transmitted,
in any form or by any means, electronic, mechanical,
photocopying, recording or otherwise, without the prior
permission of David & Charles (Publishers) Limited.

Typeset by Trade Linotype Limited, Birmingham
and printed in Great Britain by
Redwood Burn Limited, Trowbridge & Esher
for David & Charles (Publishers) Limited
Brunel House   Newton Abbot   Devon

Published in the United States of America
by David & Charles Inc
North Pomfret   Vermont 05053   USA

Contents

List of Illustrations

7

The illustration at the beginning of each chapter was drawn by Jill Allonby.

1 Breaking Through

After more than a hundred years of Test Match cricket names now abound of players who could be placed in that often quoted category 'the all-time greats'. The list is assuming unmanageable proportions, more confusing because no two people are alike in their choice of cricketers. That is only human nature but, notwithstanding the vagaries of public or private opinion, there is one aspect of the subject that has remained more or less constant over the years, with only a few minor fluctuations. Namely, that the players who would gain universal acceptance on any 'all-time' list have invariably tended to come from three countries: England, Australia and West Indies.

This does not mean that teams from India, Pakistan or New Zealand have been totally devoid of class players. They have produced many fine cricketers but far fewer than from the three first-named countries. A brief glance at the record book substantiates this. Pakistan and New Zealand have yet to produce a batsman who has accumulated an aggregate of 4,000 or more Test runs during his career. As regards India, it was not until 1979 (after nearly fifty years of Test cricket) that two batsmen succeeded in scaling the 4,000-run summit:

9

Sunil Gavaskar, rapidly followed by Gundappa Vishwanath Yet, England have thirteen, Australia eight and West Indies five.

From that one illustration it is not difficult to see why India, Pakistan and New Zealand have generally been regarded as the poor relations of Test cricket. Their players of true world-class calibre have been too few and far between to assist the teams to make a definite impact on cricket at the highest level. The only divergence from the pattern is once again supplied by India who, in the early 1970s, did enjoy a brief three-year period when there was some justification in their claim to be the premier Test side in the world at that time. Significantly, at the time India threatened the three major cricketing powers, a batsman appeared in their ranks who, almost overnight, made the rest of the world sit up and take notice.

Sunil Manohar Gavaskar was not the sole reason for India's rise from cricket obscurity; superb spin bowling was a prime factor but with the emergence of a truly world-class opening batsman from India came a rare cricketing moment. Here was a batsman who could set new standards and records that had previously not been thought possible simply because he played for one of the 'lesser' countries. Sunil Gavaskar disproved the theory and, in time, was to become the most prolific run-scorer in the history of Indian cricket.

India had previously been served by many good batsmen since first beginning to play Test cricket in 1932: Lala Amanath, Vinoo Mankad, Hazare, Manjrekar, Umrigar and Mansur Ali Khan (formerly Pataudi) fall easily from the pen but never before had an Indian batsman shown the consistency of Gavaskar over a lengthy period of time. Nor had they accumulated runs and centuries in the same profusion or speed (in terms of numbers of Tests played) as Gavaskar. Once established as a recognised Test batsman Sunil proceeded to rewrite most of the Indian Test record book and added a number of world records to his name at the same time. India had at last discovered a batsman capable of challenging nearly every batting record of any consequence at Test level. To the devotees of Bradman, Hutton, Sobers etc., the claim may sound presumptuous but the following pages will strive to provide the proof. Hopefully, by the end of the final chapter the achievements of Sunil Gavaskar will be seen to be worthy of mention in the same breath as Bradman, Hutton and other immortals of the game.

To start at the beginning it is necessary to go back in time to 10 July 1949. On that day Sunil made his entry into the world in a Bombay hospital. There was nothing particularly unusual; he arrived in much the same way as millions of babies before him but for Sunil there was one difference which could have altered the course of Indian cricket, as well his own life, completely and it happened on the very day he was born. A visitor to the hospital that day to see the new arrival was a relative, Mr Narayan Masurekar, who noticed a small hole at the top of Sunil's left ear-lobe. The mark was to be providential. The next day Nan-Kaka, as Sunil affectionately calls him, visited the hospital again but the baby he picked up from the cot next to Mrs Gavaskar's bed did not have any distinguishing feature on the left ear-lobe. Amid growing consternation and alarm a search of all the cribs in the hospital produced a happy outcome. Sunil was discovered, complete with aperture, sleeping serenely without a care in the world beside the bed of a fisherwoman.

The confusion arose after the babies had been given a bath but, if the sharp eyes of Nan-Kaka had not spotted the tiny hole in Sunil's ear, one of the premier opening batsmen in world cricket would probably have become a fisherman. By virtue of a timely intervention from fate, chance or whatever else it may be called, Sunil retained his true identity. The thousands who have since thrilled to his majestic strokeplay can be thankful for it. Sunil Gavaskar might never once have

11

lifted a blade of willow in defence of his wicket in a single cricket match, let alone a Test Match, but in the words of the old adage it was a case of 'all's well that ends well'. Sunil returned to his mother's side and the forces that seemed predestined to make him into a top-line cricketer were at work almost from the moment he was born.

In his early days there was no lack of encouragement for the aspiring young cricketer. The game was in the Gavaskar blood. Madhav Mantri, who made four Test appearances for India in the early 1950s, was Sunil's uncle while his father was an extremely capable club cricketer. No less important was the part played by Sunil's mother. She was instrumental in helping her son take his first tentative steps into cricket. Every day at home she would bowl to him and the occasion when he almost broke his mother's nose with a tennis ball has always remained firmly fixed in his memory. The daily game took place in the gallery of the house and one day Sunil played the ball straight back to his mother with some force, hitting her squarely on the nose. As the gallery was small, there was no great distance between the pair, thus increasing the force of the blow. His mother's nose began to bleed profusely but, undaunted, she merely washed her face and carried on with the game.

It was encouragement and devotion such as this that shaped Sunil's cricketing future and he has never forgotten it. When his book *Sunny Days* was published in India his gratitude was summarised graphically and simply with the touching dedication 'To Aai-Baba, My Parents'. In five words he gave all the thanks necessary and the dedication is a perfect example of the modesty and warmness of Sunil Gavaskar himself.

Apart from daily practice sessions with his mother, another of Sunil's favourite childhood pastimes was to go to his uncle's house. There, he would gaze wistfully at the many trophies and souvenirs won by Madhav Mantri. In particular, the All-India pullovers had a peculiar attraction. Sunil would caress them longingly until one day he plucked up the courage to ask his uncle if he could have one. As his uncle had so many Sunhil did not think he would mind. The answer was swift and negative. Madhav Mantri told his nephew that a cricketer had to *earn* the All-India colours and if he wanted an Indian pullover then he too would have to work, and work very hard, for the honour. It was a lesson Sunil never forgot.

There could be no easy route or short-cut to the top and with his uncle's quite proper refusal a burning desire to succeed came into Sunil's heart. Not too many years later the wisdom of Madhav Mantri's words were evident to all and the fruits of Sunil's diligent labours were a rich harvest of runs for both Bombay and India.

Sunil's education did not suffer at the expense of cricket and it began in earnest of St Xavier's High School. Cricket held a high priority in the sporting curriculum and he first played schools cricket during the 1961–2 season. By the 1963–4 season Sunil had gained selection for the Bombay Schools team but in the early days there was little success. Poor fielding caused him to be dropped from the school team. This brought about a conscious effort to improve an important element of his game. As a result, Sunil quickly developed into a specialist slip fielder, which in turn took him eventually into the slip cordon of India's Test team. Thus, in his earliest teenage years, Sunil was showing the same application and determination that was to be such a dominant feature of his later career.

Concentration has always been regarded as one of the most notable elements of Sunil's batting. He firmly believes it is no less important when fielding in the slips and because his powers of concentration are so intense he regards it as a major asset in helping him keep going even when there is little chance of a ball being edged.

Sunil regained his place in the school side and gradually began to show greater powers with the bat. The season 1965–6 (his last year at school) was by far the best in terms of achievement with scores of 246 not out, 222 and 85 in various stages of the Cooch-Behar Trophy. The undefeated double century formed part of a massive opening partnership of 421 runs and this prodigious high scoring led inevitably to Sunil's gaining selection for the All-India Schools Team to play against the touring London Schoolboys side. Concurrent with that honour came Sunil's first prize in any of the national competitions for young cricketers. He became the proud holder of the J. C. Mukherjee Trophy as the 'Best Schoolboy Cricketer of the Year'. It was 1966 and the time was rapidly approaching for Sunil to make his first-class debut.

As if to underline his claim for higher recognition Sunil scored 116 in the first match against the London Schoolboys. There were five 'Tests' in all, of which Sunil played in four, and at the end of the series he had an aggregate of 309 runs. This was Sunil's final year at school with university as the next step up the academic ladder but before beginning his studies he spent a month at a special coaching camp at Hyderabad. This was organised by the Indian Board of Control with the ex-England player T. S. Worthington as chief coach. The month-long exercise was time well spent and some important adjustments were made to Sunil's technique. It meant that he missed the first ten days of college life but shows that the India selectors were watching him closely even at the tender age of seventeen.

It was to be two years before Sunil finally made his first-class debut. In the interim period he was always apparently on the verge of selection for Bombay, being named as a member for the Ranji Trophy squad. As substitute he only fielded but after just one match Sunil was dropped from the original fourteen and he did not regain his reserve place until the following season, 1967–8. Again, he did not play in any Ranji Trophy matches but he did gain a place in the Bombay side to play the Rest of India in the annual Irani Cup match. Under the prevailing circumstances this was rather ironic. The Indian team to tour Australia and New Zealand during

14

the 1967–8 season was to be announced after this match. Consequently, while virtually everybody else playing in the match was trying to gain a place in the national side, Sunil was striving desperately to earn a place in Bombay's team.

The debut was made but recognition still lay some way ahead in the future. Despite six Bombay players taking part in the Australasian tour, Sunil was omitted from the team for the Ranji Trophy matches that followed. He was very disappointed, feeling at the time that he should have been given another chance after the Irani Cup game, even though he had failed to trouble the scorers in the second innings. Later, Sunil realised it had been a wise move on the part of the selectors. Another failure at that very early stage of his career could have had a devastating effect on his confidence. Instead, the move was positive rather than detrimental in its effect on his eventual cricketing maturation.

Two years elapsed from going to university to making his debut for Bombay and it was not until another season had passed that Sunil once again played first-class cricket. To him, it was very confusing. For the 1967–8 Ranji Trophy matches one of the players Bombay recalled was Madhav Apte, a former Test player of the early 1950s. However, he retired from the game at the end of that season, in the company of other experienced players such as Nadkarni, Hardikar and Baloo Gupte. For years they had been the backbone of the Bombay side and with their departure the door was suddenly open, with a surprising number of vacancies in the team for the 1968–9 season.

The opportunity for Sunil still did not materialise but the following year it did and, by an odd quirk of circumstance, the recall came at a time when he was not playing particularly well at university. He had been batting in great style in the university tournament a year earlier, when he had been overlooked, but—such are the ways of selectors—he had to wait until the 1969–70 season for the much desired chance to prove his worth.

The one unfortunate aspect of Sunil's Ranji Trophy debut against Mysore (now called Karnataka) was that Madhav Mantri was a member of the Bombay selection committee. Sunil opened the batting with Ashok Mankad, a former university team-mate who had already played Test cricket, but after facing just five deliveries was lbw without scoring. The reaction of the crowd had a profound effect on Sunil. The memory remains vivid of how they jeered and accused him of gaining a place solely because of his uncle's influence. It was a ridiculous idea because, whenever Sunil's name arose at selection meetings, Madhav Mantri would not take part in any debate which ensued. The average cricket follower in Bombay would not believe that and as a result Sunil became the target for the crowd's displeasure, not only when failing against Mysore but on numerous other occasions also.

Sunil's personal reaction to his dismal Ranji debut was a little strange: he returned to a completely silent dressing-room, where the other players ignored him, and while taking off his pads suddenly burst into fits of laughter! Not unnaturally, his team-mates thought Sunil had turned a trifle mad but when he explained how he had missed a simple half-volley and a golden opportunity to make runs all was revealed. It is sometimes preached that it is better to laugh than to cry. Perhaps Sunil proved the proverb true in that Bombay dressing-room in 1970.

Bombay's next Ranji Trophy match was against Rajasthan from India's Central Zone. Sunil did not expect to keep his place but, although he had failed with the batting against Mysore, he had held three slip catches and this may have influenced the selectors into persevering with the newcomer. Whatever their reasons, Sunil knew that the game against Rajasthan was a last chance to assert his claim to a regular place. He had to wait some time to bat. Rajasthan batted first, totalling 217 all out and on the second day Sunil announced his arrival in Indian first-class cricket in no uncertain manner. In partnership with Ashok Mankad, he grasped the nettle with both

16

1 Sunil Gavaskar square cuts R. A. Hutton to the boundary during the 2nd Test at Old Trafford, 1971.

2 *(left)* A fan rushes on to the pitch to congratulate Sunil Gavaskar on reaching his 50 at Old Trafford.

3 *(below)* The England slips throw up their hands as Sunil Gavaskar is caught behind by Alan Knott off the bowling of J. S. Price for 57.

hands. Each hit a century, taking the total past Rajasthan's 217 without being parted and Sunil finally fell to a catch behind the wicket, for 114, with 279 runs on the board. The date was April 1970, the match only his fourth in first-class cricket and though one swallow does not make a summer there was now every hope that the new Bombay opener could climb to success in Indian cricket.

The Indian Test selectors were taking a decided interest in Sunil by this time, although he was still a relative novice in first-class cricket. Earlier in the same season (1969–70) he had played for the Combined Universities against the touring New Zealanders. This brought him into opposition with bowlers who were faster than medium-pace for the first time in his career. Without making a large score Sunil batted soundly enough to suggest he was capable of making the transition to international cricket. The Test selectors were obviously of the same mind, for some time later they summoned Sunil to attend a trial on the fourth day of the First Test against Australia, who followed the Kiwis to India for a full-length, five-Test tour.

No Test place was found for Sunil then or during the subsequent Tests against the Aussies but by now, at the age of twenty, it was merely a matter of time before he was selected to play for India in a Test Match. The questions to answer were where, when and against whom? For the answers Sunil had to wait until the following season, 1970–1, which he began by playing for the Indian universities team on a tour of Sri Lanka. There he learnt that he had been selected by Bombay for the opening Ranji Trophy match of the season. Being on tour meant he had to miss the match and on returning home Sunil was most disappointed to discover he had been demoted to reserve for the second Ranji game against Gujarat.

Dismay turned to joy when, on the morning of the game, the captain, Ajit Wadekar, was unfit to play. Sunil filled the breach perfectly, scoring 104 with the aid of Wadekar's pads! As a reserve Sunil had seen no reason to take his own pads to the ground. When vice captain Dilip Sardesai gave Sunil the good tidings he had to telephone home and ask his mother to dash to the ground with his pads. This she did but Wadekar, seeing Sunil's problem offered his pads and when Sunil came off at lunch with 71 runs to his name his advice was simple. Don't change pads! The century resulted and Sunil was on top of the world.

The next Ranji match was against Maharashtra. Again injury came to Sunil's aid as, with Wadekar fit once more, there was a possibility he could be omitted but Sardesai cracked a rib and his place was safe. Of all his early Ranji Trophy appearances Sunil classed this match as the most critical to his personal cricketing fortunes. Failure in it would undoubtedly have caused a severe set-back to his aspirations but Sunil was not prepared to let any chances go begging now. An innings of 176 was his third Ranji Trophy century in as many matches. Following the failure in his first appearance against Mysore the doubts were now dispelled. Sunil was firmly established as batsman of the future and his three centuries in 1970 (spread over two seasons, 1969–70 and 1970–1) produced repeated prophecies that he would be selected for the forthcoming Indian tour of West Indies, due to commence in the early months of 1971.

Sunil was not quite as optimistic as his friends and fellow players. He had been playing extremely well in the Ranji Trophy but, following the Maharashtra match, he was not included in the West Zone side to play South Zone in the Duleep Trophy. This was another disappointment to an often bewildered young player. It was all well and good for people to make confident predictions about the West Indies tour but, with only five first-class appearances to his name, Sunil harboured the secret fear that inexperience would count against him in the final reckoning of the selectors.

After consultation with Madhav Mantri Sunil decided to put the pressure of impending international honours to the back of his mind and went to Poona to captain the Bombay Universities there in the inter-university matches. Pressure or otherwise, there appeared to be nothing wrong with Sunil's batting as he made scores of 226, 99, 327 and 124. Although these were not first-class games, he gave a glorious exhibition of batting and the triple century broke a twelve-year-old record established by Ajit Wadekar (324) as the highest individual score in the university tournament. The Bombay University side duly reached the semi-final stage of the All-India University Championship and the day that the university players left for Waltair to compete in the finals the players chosen to go to West Indies were to be announced.

For Sunil the tension was beginning to mount. While his university team-mates travelled south to Waltair, Sunil stayed behind in Bombay to await the decision of the selectors. Most of the fateful day was spent in the company of Saeed Ahmed Hattea, another young player with high hopes of being included in the touring party. At first they went to a cinema to pass the time but were unable to sit through the film. They walked out and went to the offices of the Bombay Cricket Association in search of news. With the selection committee still in conference their nerve ends continued to jangle and the pair decided to go home. There was nothing else they could do except wait but the train journey was no tonic for Sunil's agitated mind. The commuters easily recognised Saeed with his long hair and many 'selected' him for the touring party.

'Yes, but what about Mr Gavaskar?' asked Saeed pointing to Sunil.

'OK, he will be there also', came the commuters' rather bland reply. To Sunil the statement was far from confident.

The two friends parted with a promise to telephone each other as soon as they heard any news. At home, the family atmosphere was far more relaxed than Sunil was, with the exception of his mother. She was rather tense, while father and sister remained confident that Sunil would be selected.

21

For a while he played with his cousin. As no news had arrived he decided to take the youngster home but he was barely outside the house when the telephone rang. Anxiously, Sunil waited outside, hoping the call would be for him. Within moments his trepidation was dispelled. Ashok Mankad was on the line with the news that he was in the party to go to West Indies. That was it! The young batsman from Bombay had made his mark and forced his way into international cricket at the age of twenty-one, after less than half-a-dozen first-class appearances. For Sunil, it was 'West Indies, here I come!'

The years of hard work had paid their dividend. From the earliest days when his mother bowled gentle lobs to him in the gallery of their house, on to his own strenuous practice to improve his fielding and finally through to the battle to break into Bombay's Ranji Trophy side. Each succeeding obstacle had been surmounted and now Sunil could claim the prize: his place in the touring party bound for the Caribbean. It was a success story but nobody, even in their wildest dreams, could envisage exactly how successful that was to be for Sunil. It would not merely be successful, it would be phenomenal.

2 The First Tour

Amidst all the excitement of preparing for the tour of West Indies Sunil began to experience a strange pain in the middle finger of his left hand. It first appeared three days before the team was due to leave and a doctor diagnosed the ailment as a whitlow. Apparently, it was nothing untoward. Apart from causing Sunil to miss a few days' net practice there was no cause for alarm. Team-mate Govindraj had also suffered the same trouble and gave Sunil a remedy to cure the niggling pain, although at that stage Sunil continued to follow the doctor's instructions only.

Here was another example of the external forces which influenced, guided and generally chaperoned Sunil's career. As twenty-one years earlier, a chance peek at the ear of a new-born baby had ensured that the real Sunil Gavaskar went home from hospital with his mother, similarly with his finger so many years later. It was to become so inflamed and swollen that there could have been far-reaching, even disastrous consequences for the young player about to embark on his Test career. In his own words, 'It could have stopped my Test career from starting at all.'

At first, the whitlow was no more than troublesome. To

prevent catching it against anybody in a crowd, Sunil band-
aged the finger for the first part of the journey to West Indies,
which was to be made via London and New York. During the
first leg of the flight he decided to follow the advice of
Govindraj whose local remedy entailed pushing the offending
finger into a piece of sliced sweet lime. According to Govindraj
this would draw the pus from the finger, lessen the pain and
then healing would follow in a very short time.

After an overnight stop in London the team flew on to
New York but by this time Sunil was in real pain. He could
not move the finger at all and the intensity of the throbbing
was causing him to shout aloud in anguish. The situation was
becoming acute. There was a hurried conversation with the
team manager, Mr Kiki Tarapor, and a special announcement was broadcast to the passengers, appealing for a doctor
to come forward. Luckily, there was one on board. He was
able to give Sunil some pain-killing capsules but although it
silenced his cries of pain the swelling continued to increase
ominously.

Once at New York, Mr Tarapor took Sunil straight to the
hospital. There, a nurse could not bear to look at the finger.
She had to turn her head away because of its swollen state
and the hospital doctor had no hesitation in deciding to
perform an immediate operation to draw the pus from the
abscess. 'I could not believe that it was my own hand', Sunil
said afterwards and that statement was too close to the truth
for comfort. The doctor said the operation would take less
than ten minutes but as a measure of how serious the consequences might have been he added, 'Thank God you've come
now. If you had delayed another twenty-four hours, gangrene
would have set in and the finger would have had to be
chopped off.'

It was a close call! Minus the middle finger of his left hand
Sunil would not have found batting particularly easy.
With the aid of the surgeon's scalpel the problem did not
arise and the matter was very soon put right. The one un-

fortunate outcome of the episode was that Sunil would miss the first three matches, including the First Test in West Indies. He lost some blood during the operation and the finger took quite some time to heal fully. It was frustrating but a small price to pay for keeping intact not only his left hand but his entire Test career.

A one-day match against the University of West Indies at Kingston, Jamaica, was Sunil's first taste of Caribbean cricket. The match took place immediately prior to the First Test, and on the same ground, but it was obvious that he would not be in contention for a Test place as he had yet to play a first-class game in West Indies. This was rectified two days after the Test ended. The match was against the Leeward Islands and, from the outset, Sunil served notice of his intentions for the remainder of the tour. India won a comfortable nine-wicket victory but, more important, was the role played by Sunil. From two innings he scored 114 runs, 82 coming at the first time of asking and his 32 in the second innings was un-defeated. The obvious skill and talent were being demonstrated at the first opportunity and with his first game safely under his belt Sunil had no intentions of resting on his laurels. In the very next game he progressed another step up the ladder of cricketing success.

The fixture was against Trinidad. Although it eventually petered out to a lifeless draw Sunil was very much in evidence throughout proceedings. In the first innings came the first of a quintet of centuries Sunil was to hit on the tour as he cracked 125 runs off the Trinidadian bowlers. For an encore, his second innings produced 63 more runs. This meant Sunil had hit over 300 runs from just four visits to the crease (once not out) since returning to fitness. In a very short space of time he had given West Indies fair warning of what was likely to happen in the remaining four Tests. Any forebodings the West Indies players may reasonably have felt at that time were to be entirely justified.

During the following two months all games would come

alike to Sunil, whether they were 'ordinary' first-class fixtures or the all-important Tests. Had it not been for the unfortunate trio of missed matches at the beginning of the tour he would surely have established all manner of records in addition to those he did make. That he did not 'sweep the board' with his record-breaking achievments does not really matter because, pleasant though it would have been for him, there was another fact concerning his batting which counted far more than mere records. Splendidly as Sunil had batted in the two Island games, those four innings would be seen later as being nothing more than workmanlike performances, when compared to the heights he would scale in the Tests—such was the impact this astonishingly talented young batsman was to make on his first tour.

Following the Trinidad game came one of the highlights of any Test cricketer's career and the fulfilment of the dream of millions of small boys around the world—that magical moment that constitutes a Test Match debut. Through missing the First Test, Sunil's moment came at Port of Spain on 6 March 1971. An international debut is a momentous occasion for any young sportsman and this description of it comes from the player himself.

'To actually play for your country is every young man's dream and I was no different', said Sunil. 'When I was told by Ajit Wadekar that I was picked for the Test I was in the heavens. The rest of the team also poured in their congratulations. My real ambition has been not only to play for my country but to play successfully. Only after I stepped on to the field at the Trinidad Oval for my Test debut did I wear the cap allotted to me for the tour.'

To play successfully was what Sunil desired. To judge success is not always as simple as it would appear. In any sphere success is related to several other factors, not least being the relative level of success attained either before or after a particular event. For example, if a batsman were to be told in advance that he would score two half-centuries on his Test debut he would probably accept it as more than satisfactory. What better start to an international career could a man ask for? Unless he was particularly vain or greedy the answer must be not very much.

With Sunil, he did make the dream start to his Test career by scoring a half-century in each innings against West Indies, the second effort being undefeated. Ironically, his later exploits made it appear as no more than a toning-up exercise. It was as if he was merely whetting his appetite against the bowling in readiness for larger helpings later on. However his initial performance is studied there can be no doubt that Sunil did make a successful entry into Test cricket but when compared against his batting in the remaining Tests it was no more than moderately successful and that is the real measure of of Sunil's overall success on the tour as a whole.

Through the luck of the toss, Sunil's first real taste of Test Match action came not with bat but with the ball. West Indies batted first and the Indian bowlers performed magnificently to dismiss the opposition for 214 runs on the first day's play. No catches went Sunil's way but he was called upon to bowl one over of leg-breaks which cost 9 runs without troubling the batsmen.

Sunil was rather glad West Indies batted first. Their innings gave him time to absorb the Test Match atmosphere and with the bowlers performing so well he had half-an-hour's play to survive to the end of play. Or, as Sunil succinctly described the occasion later, he strode to the wicket for the first time into the tough, tense atmosphere of Test cricket at 'the fag end of the day'. Somewhat amusingly, his first runs in Test cricket came to him by courtesy of the umpire because, though the ball went off his pads, he did not signal leg-byes when the runs were taken.

On the second day Sunil had the good fortune to be dropped by no less a person than Gary Sobers with just 12 runs to his name. After seeing out the new ball he began to grow in confidence and moved on to 65 before pulling a long hop to mid-wicket. Nervous or otherwise it did not show. Sunil had played with a calm assurance that belied his years and the first scorecard entry against his name was all that he, his side and his family at home could hope for. It read:

S. M. Gavaskar ct Lloyd b Noreiga 65

India were well placed at the end of the first innings. In addition to Sunil's opening effort, Sardesai hit a splendid century and Solkar added a half-century; India were well content to take a lead of 138 runs. The lead was useful but no more. Then, two entirely unconnected factors combined to virtually assure India of a victory historic in the annals of Indian cricket.

Firstly, the pitch became ideal for spin bowling, of which the Indians had top-class performers in abundance. Second, came a freak accident which robbed West Indies of a key batsman at a crucial stage of the game. Batsman Charlie Davis was practising in the nets with Roy Fredericks in an adjoining net. A ball hit by Fredericks pierced the net, ricocheted off a pole and hit Davis above the eye, causing a wound which required stitches. The batsmen had been practising before the start of play on the fourth day but, unfortunately, by the time Davis returned from the hospital to resume his innings West Indies had suffered a minor batting collapse.

At the start of play on the fourth day West Indies were 12 runs ahead for the loss of a solitary second innings wicket. Without Davis, 4 wickets fell for the addition of just 19 runs and the course of the match was virtually sealed. Bravely, Davis went back to the crease to score 74 not out, to add to his 71 not out in the first innings but, spirited though the performance was, the damage caused by the mid-order collapse was irreparable.

The West Indies second innings finished at 261 all out. Thus India had eight hours of the match remaining in which to score a modest 124 runs for an historic victory. After twenty-five Tests between the two countries, spread over twenty-three years of competition, India had a gilt-edged opportunity to record their first-ever victory over West Indies. Fittingly enough, for a man not much more than a boy playing in his first Test, Sunil was the person to see India home after a few hesitant moments as the target drew closer.

All began well, as Sunil and Ashok Mankad ably compiled an opening partnership of 74 runs. Then Mankad and Durani fell at the same score, quickly followed by Sardesai 10 runs later. These were anxious moments but Abid Ali, promoted in the order, hit boldly. The new recruit at the opposite end of the wicket remained as cool as a veteran and, with a full day to spare, the pair safely guided India to victory. This landmark in Indian cricket was the more remarkable because it was on the opposition's own territory and Sunil could feel immense pride in his own contribution. Typically, he summarised his feelings in a different way. He said, 'It has always been a matter of great pride that I was able, in my very first Test, to be associated with India's maiden Test victory over West Indies and that too in the lion's den.'

The full scorecard of India's unprecedented triumph is shown on pages 30 and 31.

While not amassing huge scores in either of his innings Sunil had displayed the ideal temperament. The complete Test batsman is a complex article, having to possess many different traits. At the Trinidad Oval Sunil was unhurried, outwardly calm and with the often awe-inspiring first appearance behind him was beginning to have a quietly growing confidence in his own ability. The future augured well for the young batsman from Bombay.

Georgetown was the setting for the Third Test. Being one up in the series it was perhaps predictable that India would be content with a draw. A stalemate became inevitable from quite early in the game but before the game was finished there were several moments of drama and high tension.

The first incident of any note came during West Indies first innings and gave Sunil another 'first' in his brief, two-Test

West Indies v India

Second Test Match 6, 7, 9, 10 & 11 March 1971 at Port of Spain, Trinidad

West Indies

Batsman	1st Innings		2nd Innings	
R. C. Fredericks	b Abid Ali	0	run out	80
G. S. Camacho	ct Solkar b Bedi	18	b Venkataraghavan	3
R. B. Kanhai	ct Solkar b Prasanna	37	ct Venkataraghavan b Bedi	27
C. H. Lloyd	b Abid Ali	7	ct Wadekar b Durani	15
C. A. Davis	not out	71	not out	74
G. S. Sobers	b Venkataraghavan	29	b Durani	0
A. G. Barrett	ct Solkar b Prasanna	8	b Venkataraghavan	19
T. M. Findlay	b Bedi	1	ct Solkar b Venkataraghavan	0
V. A. Holder	ct Krishnamurthy b Bedi	14	b Venkataraghavan	14
G. C. Shillingford	ct Solkar b Prasanna	25	ct Durani b Venkataraghavan	1
J. Noreiga	b Prasanna	0	ct Solkar b Bedi	2
Extras	b2 lb2	4	b18 lb7 nb1	26
Total		214		261

Fall of Wickets

	1	2	3	4	5	6	7	8	9
	0	42	62	62	108	132	133	161	214
	73	150	152	169	169	218	222	254	256

Bowling

	O	M	R	W	O	M	R	W
Abid Ali	20	4	52	2	5	2	3	0
Solkar	3	0	12	0	7	2	19	0
Gavaskar	1	0	9	0	—	—	—	—
Bedi	16	5	46	3	29·5	11	50	2
Prasanna	19·5	3	54	4	16	5	47	0
Venkataraghavan	13	0	35	1	36	11	95	5
Durani	—	—	—	—	17	8	21	2

India

	1st Innings		2nd Innings	
A. V. Mankad	b Shillingford	44	ct sub b Barrett	29
S. M. Gavaskar	ct Lloyd b Noreiga	65	not out	67
S. A. Durani	ct & b Noreiga	9	b Barrett	0
D. N. Sardesai	ct Shillingford b Noreiga	112	ct Findlay b Barrett	3
A. L. Wadekar	ct Kanhai b Noreiga	0		
E. D. Solkar	ct & b Noreiga	55		
S. Abid Ali	ct Shillingford b Noreiga	20	not out	21
S. Venkataraghavan	st Findlay b Noreiga	5		
P. Krishnamurthy	ct sub b Noreiga	0		
E. A. S. Prasanna	not out	10		
B. S. Bedi	ct Holder b Noreiga	4		
Extras	b18 lb2 nb8	28	b2 lb2 nb1	5
Total		352		125

Fall of Wickets

1	2	3	4	5	6	7	8	9
68	90	186	186	300	330	337	337	342
74	74	84						

Bowling

Bowling	O	M	R	W
Holder	19	8	37	0
Shillingford	20	3	45	1
Sobers	28	7	65	0
Barrett	37	13	65	0
Noreiga	49·4	16	95	9
Davis	1	1	11	0
Lloyd	1	0	6	0

Bowling	O	M	R	W
Holder	2	0	12	0
Shillingford	6	2	13	0
Sobers	15	5	16	0
Barrett	8·4	0	43	3
Noreiga	18	4	36	0

India won by 7 wickets

career. He took his first Test catch and was on a road that would take him to the eventual milestone of fifty Test catches. Eknath Solkar (a team-mate in West Indies) with 53 catches was the only Indian player, other than a wicketkeeper, to take more than fifty catches in Tests and with the passing of time that record too would fall into Sunil's hands. The first catch was K. D. Boyce ct Gavaskar b Venkataraghavan 9.

More was to come from Sunil when India replied to the West Indies total of 363 all out. He batted in superb, masterful form. To some extent he was fortunate, being dropped twice before reaching 50, but he made the most of his good luck. In a stay at the crease lasting four hours twenty minutes Sunil moved sweetly towards his first Test century. It duly materialised and he progressed to 116 before falling to Sobers. There appeared to be little West Indies could do to stop the prodigy from scoring! The century effectively ensured that India would reach West Indies first innings total, which they did pass, albeit by the slender margin of 13 runs, but by that time the game was well into the fourth day. At close of play West Indies were 63 for 1 wicket leaving little scope for any result other than a draw. Although the result was a foregone conclusion the game was far from finished.

On the final day West Indies progressed to 137 for 3 wickets, at which point Sobers went to the crease. Within minutes a flashpoint situation occurred that was surrounded by controversy. Sobers played forward to Durani and there was an immediate appeal for a bat–pad catch at short-leg. The appeal was so confident it was repeated when the first shout was turned down. The second request suffered a similar rejection and at this juncture Durani made known his feelings by hurling the ball to the ground in utter disgust. From Sunil's position at long-on there appeared to have been a clear deflection from the bat but, as Sobers held his ground waiting for the decision, Sunil also thought there must have been some doubt. 'Gary has always been a "walker" ', Sunil said, 'and so perhaps he knew best.'

One way or another the decision sealed the fate of the game. Sobers, with Davis as his partner, raised the total by 170 runs. Both hit centuries and at tea Sobers made a rather meaningless declaration, setting India a target of 294 runs to win in ninety minutes.It was impossible but Sunil and Ashok Mankad were not deterred from indulging in some splendid, free-hitting batting practice. By close they had rattled the score along to 123 without being parted and, with both hitting undefeated half-centuries, the match had once again proved an unmitigated success for Sunil.

Four innings in two Tests had thus far produced one century and three half-centuries. On two occasions the bowlers failed to remove Sunil from the crease and already his Test average was beginning to assume gigantic proportions. As always, with a story-book start to a career such as Sunil was experiencing, there had to be a question mark. In his case, it was not whether he was good enough to fulfil his appointed role. It was quite the opposite. Was it possible, for one so young and inexperienced in Test cricket, to maintain this amazing spate of high scores?

The Fourth Test was played at Bridgetown, where Sunil made his one and only negligible score of the series. The game was a strange mixture, with West Indies holding the advantage for one of the few times in the entire series but by close of play on the last day India had saved the match comfortably. A draw was exactly what Indian sought and this was made clear by Wadekar when he put West Indies in to bat. Sobers did not waste the opportunity, scoring 178 not out in a total of 501 for 5 wickets declared. There was an hour's play left when Sobers declared and in what time remained (bad light curtailed the final session) India were quickly in trouble.

Sunil was the batsman to fall, mistiming a hook at a bumper from Dowe. Holder held the catch and, with Sunil dismissed for a single, India began to struggle. On the third day the innings was crumbling at 70 for 6 wickets when

Solkar joined Sardesai to effectively ensure a draw for India. The seventh wicket partnership added 186 runs to the total. To avoid the follow-on was the target and without the brilliant combined efforts of Solkar and Sardesai the goal would not have been reached, though notwithstanding the fine partnership the target should still have been beyond India's grasp. With the last pair at the wicket Dowe failed to run-out a helplessly stranded Bedi and from there the mercurial spin-bowler went on to assist Sardesai compile a record-breaking partnership of 62. Sardesai was last out, for a marvellous 150, and as a result of his efforts India were almost safe from defeat. Almost, but not quite. Solkar and Bedi had batted staunchly with the 'Sardee Maan', as West Indies supporters affectionately nicknamed Sardesai, but more resolute batting was still required in the second innings.

But first West Indies quickly scored 180 for 6 wickets, at which point Sobers declared after only one over on the last day. With a whole day's play remaining, minus a few minutes, India were far from certain of escaping with a draw but Sunil reigned supreme. For him, the crucial factor was West Indies' lack of an off-spinner to utilise the rough patches caused by the bowlers' follow-through. The task was therefore simplified slightly and Sunil batted throughout the rest of the day.

When the match ended Sunil was still at the crease with 117 runs to his credit out of a total of 221 for 5 wickets. His concentration had been impeccable in a flawless innings, proving once again that India had discovered a batsman of the highest calibre. Sunil was undoubtedly in brilliant form but after what he had already achieved in the Tests it was difficult to imagine him improving further. Two centuries in three Tests were as much as anybody could expect from him. Except, that is, Sunil himself. He was far from finished and with one Test remaining he was about to enter the cricket record books in a fashion only once before equalled in Test cricket and only twice since. Thus, in only his fourth Test appearance, Sunil was to join the select band of players who

4 Sunil Gavaskar, watched by the Indian wicket-keeper Farouk Engineer, catches Keith Fletcher in the slips off the bowling of Bedi. This was Gavaskar's second catch during the England 1st Innings at the Oval, 1971.

5 Play is held up at the Oval as a dog runs towards Sunil Gavaskar.

6 & 7 *(above left)* Sunil Gavaskar's middle stump is removed by John Snow during India's first innings at the Oval, 1971; *(above right)* Sunil Gavaskar demonstrates the controlled power and technique which has made him one of the world's most consistent opening batsmen.

8 *(below)* Playing for a Rest of the World side against Victoria in 1971, Gavaskar despatches Alan 'Froggy' Thompson to the boundary.

form unique 'clubs' by virtue of exceptional performances.

The final Test was played at a ground of happy memories for Sunil: Port of Spain's Trinidad Oval. His entry into Test cricket had been made there and there would be little to change the sequence of events in this game, which was extended to six days as the series was still open, with India holding just a slender one–nil lead. Winning the toss, India batted first. That a total of 360 all out was reached was due very largely to a marathon effort from Sunil, lasting six hours forty minutes. In a flawless display he held the Indian innings together, scoring 124 priceless runs, special assistance coming from Sardesai with 75 in a third wicket stand of 122 runs but the general consensus of opinion was that the total would not be sufficient for a six-day match.

Unless something drastic happened during the West Indies first innings, it appeared that the best India could hope for was a draw. When West Indies did not fail and duly took a sizeable lead even the drawn result became a rapidly receding possibility but India had one trump card still to play—Sunil Gavaskar. In this, his final Test innings of the tour, Sunil was to outstrip everything he had previously accomplished. His name could go straight into the record books and for his team the outcome was that not only had the game been saved but, because of his second innings, India very nearly completed a remarkable victory over West Indies.

The bare facts of the innings show that Sunil batted for eight hours fifty minutes, scored 220 runs before being bowled by Shepherd and was only the second batsman to score a century and a double century in the same Test. K. D. Walters, of Australia, was the first, also against West Indies at Sydney, scoring 242 and 103 in 1968–9, although L. G. Rowe of the West Indies, and G. S. Chappell of Australia, also accomplished the feat later. The statistics do not tell the whole story and for both innings it is remarkable.

Whilst practising before the fifth Test began, Sunil had taken a drink of iced water which contained a small piece of unmelted ice. This had fallen into a cavity in a tooth and the result was excruciating pain. Over the following five days Sunil suffered agony but as the Test was under way he could neither have the tooth extracted nor take pain-killing tablets. Thus both innings were completed under considerable duress but the double century was a truly tremendous performance because by then Sunil was very weak from lack of sleep and food caused by the aching tooth. When it was finally extracted Gundappa Vishwanath suggested Sunil should keep the tooth as a memento of his six days and nights of torment and ecstasy. He did not. The memory alone was sufficient!

Sunil's performance can be measured from two separate viewpoints: the next highest score in India's second innings total of 427 all out was 54 by Ajit Wadekar and he was only the second Indian player to score a century in each innings of a Test, following in the steps of V. S. Hazare twenty-four years earlier against Australia. However the performance is viewed, it was a monumental effort on Sunil's part, well worth the ecstatic standing ovation he received from the crowd at the Trinidad Oval at the end of his second innings.

In the final reckoning, Sunil's batting very nearly gave India a startling victory. West Indies required 212 runs to win in little more than two and a half hours. The target was possible though not probable and when, at the close, West Indies were hanging on grimly at 165 for 8 wickets the game was all but lost. It was a case of so near, yet so far but India would have few qualms about the eventual draw. They had won the series by one–nil and the tour had been quite easily India's most successful foray overseas in thirty-nine years of Test cricket. Only once previously had an Indian team triumphed away from home, three–one against New Zealand in 1967–8, but in that instance the standard of the opposition was not in the same league as West Indies.

There ended Sunil's first Test series. When the facts and figures were analysed his achievements were breath-taking. Suddenly his name stood comparison with cricket's legends of the past. In four Tests he had scored 774 runs while in all first-class matches the aggregate was 1,169. The Tests provided eight innings, in which he scored one double century, three centuries and three half centuries. There, in simple terms, were his achievements and they were the main reason for the name of Gavaskar receiving rapturous attention throughout the cricketing world. There were six important reasons for this:

1 Sunil had established a new record for the highest aggregate in a maiden Test series, beating the previous record of 703 set by G. A. Headley in 1929–30 v England.
2 No Indian batsman had previously scored 700 runs or more in a Test series.
3 Only K. D. Walters before him had scored a century and a double century in the same Test.
4 Only two players, E. H. Hendren and A. Sandham, had previously scored more runs in a West Indies season.
5 Only one other batsman in cricket history had finished a Test series with a higher average than the 154·80 attained by Sunil—none other than the incomparable Sir Donald Bradman with 201·50 v South Africa in 1931–2 and 178·75 v India in 1947–8.
6 Sunil failed by just 5 runs to equal the aggregate of 779 by E. D. Weekes, which was the record for a India–West Indies series.

Sunil had set or approached numerous records and, but for missing the First Test, he would surely have passed E. D. Weekes's aggregate of 779 runs for the series. Typically, Sunil did not take such an optimistic view. 'Oh, I don't know', he said, 'I could have been bowled first ball.' It was customary modesty from a player who had set out for West Indies with the simple wish: 'I would have been happy if I had not made a fool of myself.' When considering India's somewhat delicate record against pace bowling (of which West Indies had a plentiful supply) Sunil's performance on his first tour was staggering. India now possessed two batsmen who could stand up to the fastest bowling of any country.

The second was Gundappa Vishwanath who, although just six months older than Sunil, had started his Test career in November 1969, eighteen months prior to the Caribbean tour. In time, their careers were to progress along much the same successful route. In 1971, Vishwanath already had a high reputation, although he had a quiet series against West Indies, and, with the emergence of Sunil into world ranks, the future for Indian cricket was as bright as it had ever been since Test status had been granted so many years earlier.

Inevitably, Sunil's meteoric rise to success would pose a number of questions. Had everything happened too early, and too quickly in his career? But Sunil was to go from strength to strength, approaching records, breaking them and attaining a stature unparalleled in Indian cricket—but that lay well into the future. In the meantime, it was particularly noticeable that, following his 220 against West Indies, Sunil would bat in another seventeen Test innings before registering another century. In terms of time and Tests, that meant three years and more, or another nine Tests, before another hundred would come his way. It is a sobering thought that, while his class was indisputable, time was a vital factor in its development. Until he matured, Sunil's rare talents would not flourish again as in West Indies but the final Sunil Gavaskar would return eventually to his Caribbean form with a vengeance. Not only return, but surpass it.

Averages for 1971 series v. West Indies, 5 Tests, played 4

Tests	Inns	NO	Runs	HS	Average	Bowling: 1–0–9–0
4	8	3	774	220	154·80	Fielding: 1 ct

Results: West Indies 0, India 1, 4 Tests drawn

3 Back to Earth

The return to India was tumultuous. Indian cricket supporters are fanatical and after the unprecedented Caribbean victory the team fully expected a huge gathering to greet them at Bombay's Santa Cruz airport. True to tradition, the players were accorded a heroes' welcome. Unfortunately, the reverse can apply equally when the results are not in India's favour. In the words of Sunil, when the team played less than well, public reaction could be 'unbelievably bad'. Exactly what this meant will be seen later but, for the moment, everything was perfect. Garlands of flowers, handshakes and tributes poured in from all corners of India to the nation's most successful team ever to venture abroad.

The celebrations were, of necessity, short-lived. The team were very soon reassembling and busily preparing for a short three-Test tour of England that would begin in June 1971, Sunil's place in the party was assured. With a Test average of 150-plus it had to be but, quite naturally, it was not expected that he would maintain his supercharged rate of run-scoring. It was not humanly possible. A more feasible prospect was that India's team as a whole could possibly perform as successfully as on their previous mission. With this in mind, Professor Chandgadkar, then president of the Indian Board of Control, gave the players a promise immediately before the departure for London. If they could achieve the same level of success against England as against West Indies, a red-carpet welcome would greet the players on their return which would stretch from Santa Cruz airport to Bombay's Brabourne Stadium.

It was understandable that the team should be buoyantly confident in view of the recent past. However, if previous encounters with England were anything to take into account the odds were heavily against the Indians. In the first instance, India had never won a solitary Test Match in England during any of their six previous visits to the country!

On known form, when competing in England, India's chances had to be rated as very slender indeed except for the morale-boosting victory over West Indies a few months earlier. A most cursory of glances at the facts and figures proves the point to be true. In thirty-nine years of Test competition, from 1932, the two teams had met on thirty-seven occasions, nineteen in England and eighteen in India. The records India produced at home and abroad provide stark contrast.

India had recorded three victories at home (one in 1951–2 and two in 1963–4), compared to three defeats with the remaining dozen games drawn. A high proportion of drawn games is the rule rather than the exception on the subcontinent and, overall, India had fared reasonably well in four home series against England. Only one rubber had been lost outright, in 1933–4, when the scoreline was 0–2 with one Test drawn. The next series to be played was in 1951–2, bringing about India's first success over England and the eventual result was a 1–1 drawn series, with three Tests undecided.

Following a break of ten years, England returned to India in 1961–2, when all five Tests ended in stalemate. Two years later E. R. Dexter led another team east, probably the strongest England team yet to be sent to India. They were surprisingly beaten by 2–0. This was a real highlight in the history of Indian cricket. It is true that bowlers of the calibre of Trueman and Statham did not go on the tour but this detracts little from the Indian performance. They had won and won convincingly. Thus, at home, the results were favourable. Yet in England the story was near humiliation.

Six separate series, comprising eighteen Tests, had failed to produce a single Indian victory and in two of the series England's superiority had been overwhelming. In mitigation, it was to the eternal bad luck of the Indian batsmen that during the two series in question, 1952 and 1959, they had faced the full fury of a rampant Fred Trueman. Not surprisingly, India lost eight of the nine Tests played in those years. The picture was little brighter when considering the remaining four series. In all, England had registered fifteen victories with four drawn games as the only crumb of comfort for India. The full playing record read as follows: *P* 37 *W* 3 *D* 16 *L* 18; in England the figures were: *P* 19 *W* 0 *D* 4 *L* 15.

In the light of past statistics, India's hopes were anything but bright and a similar forecast could be made on current form. England were enjoying a hitherto unprecedented purple patch, having gone a record twenty-three Tests without defeat before the 1971 series began. A measure of how well England were playing can be gleaned from the fact that while India were successfully competing in West Indies, England were similarly engaged against the might of Australia at very much the same time. An Ashes battle is always particularly sternly contested and after a gap of twelve years England had finally wrested the trophy back from the Aussies. Having won 2–0, in a marathon seven-Test series, England had a justifiable claim to the title of cricket's premier side. Top team or not, there was still a tiny glimmer of hope for the Indian tourists.

In between the completion of the Australasian tour and the beginning of the home series with India, England received

Pakistan as visitors for a similar shortened three-Test series. The first two matches were undecided but in the third game England barely scraped home to victory, the final margin being a meagre 25 runs. The result proved that England were far from invincible, despite the impressive record of the recent past. Also, India were fielding what was probably their strongest-ever team and there was no doubt that they were in splendid form when the series began in June. If Pakistan could closely contest a series with England, India could do exactly the same with a side arguably much superior.

There were many intriguing questions awaiting answers as the tour got under way. Could it be, after so many years in the cricketing wilderness, that India were about to spring a major surprise and perform in a manner far different to previous English tours? For the answers, the pundits would have to wait until August. In the meantime, there would be sufficient tension, drama, excitement and controversy to keep everybody guessing as to the outcome. Of the four ingredients, controversy came first. As a result, Sunil became the centre of attention in that sphere for the first, but certainly not the last, time in his career.

The furore erupted during the second innings of the First Test at Lords, with Sunil the central figure in an ugly and unsporting incident. Much had gone before and at that stage the match was very evenly poised. When rain washed out the remaining hours of play on the final day, the position was evenly balanced. A result either way would definitely have been reached for India required just 38 runs to win but had only 2 wickets remaining when the heavens opened. England probably held a slight advantage but once again they had been pushed to the limit.

England had taken strike first, totalling 304 all out, to which India replied with 313 all out. Sunil's contribution was a modest 4 but it was in the second innings that his name made the headlines—and not for any feats of high scoring. Batting a second time, England were dismissed for 191

44

thereby setting India a target of 183 runs and at this juncture Sunil unwittingly became involved in the most controversial affair of the entire 1971 English season.

What took place at Lords was not caused by Sunil's hand. The 'Snow Incident' (as the event was christened by the nation's press) happened when he was at the non-striker's end of the wicket and the action involved was very straight-forward. Paceman John Snow was bowling and when a short, sharp single was called for, both Sunil and Snow began running up the wicket together. Apparently without justification at all, and with no regard for sportsmanship Snow knocked Sunil to the ground from behind, with a shoulder-charge any footballer would have been proud of. As the venue was Lords and not Wembley the uproar was immediate.

The incident received blanket coverage in the press and on television, giving cricket publicity of the worst possible kind. For his pains, Snow was summarily dropped from the England team for the Second Test, which at least showed what the selectors thought of his actions. In addition, he was made to apologise to Sunil personally by the chairman of selectors and the secretary of the TCCB. It was a flagrant breach of decent cricketing conduct and the later MCC actions left no doubt as to what they thought of the matter.

Sunil thought the whole affair was blown-up out of all pro-portion to the actual event on the field. At a time, a partner-ship was developing which was causing the England bowlers some anxiety. Sunil could see that Snow was becoming exasperated and that when the quick single was called for the bowler over-reacted. To make the incident appear far worse than may have actually been the case, there was the difference in size between the two men. If Sunil had been nearer to Snow's 6-foot bulk he might only have stumbled but not fallen, and in that event Sunil had a shrewd idea of what might have taken place.

'If I was a six-footer like him, maybe Snow would not have tried that then', said Sunil philosophically, but there was a mischievous twinkle in his eyes as he gave his views on the subject. No amount of probing could elicit further comment from Sunil and there the matter ended, closed with a handshake in a Lords dressing-room in 1971.

Apart from enduring the soccer-style antics of Snow, Sunil gave a very polished display in the second innings at Lords. Batting for two hours, he scored 53 before falling to the spin of Gifford. Sunil demonstrated his style, poise and technique exceptionally well in difficult, wet, cold conditions. In the process the knock was instrumental in saving India from defeat. He was sixth out, at 114, on the fifth day and by the tea interval two more wickets fell. With the advent of rain an enthralling encounter was washed out as a draw.

The Second Test at Old Trafford was also affected by the weather, no play at all being possible on the last day. England appeared to hold the upper hand although rain was always imminent throughout the game and it came as no surprise when the final deluge sealed the result. In the first England innings Sunil enjoyed a particularly fine time in the field taking three catches. Of the trio, the effort to dismiss Illingworth gave Sunil most pleasure. The England captain had scored a century when he drove hard at a half-volley from Venkataraghavan. The ball flew hard and fast to the left of Sunil in the slips where he clung on to a brilliant catch.

England reached 386 all out, to which India replied with 212, a total that was a mere 26 runs more than was required to avert the follow-on. In fact, without half-centuries from Sunil and Eknath Solkar the follow-on would not have been saved. Of the two innings, Sunil's 57 was quite remarkable. Batting for the eleventh time in a Test Match in his short career Sunil had now passed the half-century mark on no less than nine occasions. It was staggering consistency from a player of his limited experience, although he was not making the extremely large scores of the West Indies tour. A comparative Test novice, little more than twenty-two years of age, he had been playing top-class cricket non-stop for almost a whole year. Such consistency from one so young and in-experienced proves Sunil's fierce concentration and determin-ation to perform to the best of his ability, whenever he wears an All-India cricket cap.

England took a sizeable first innings lead at Old Trafford. It amounted to 174 runs and was capitalised on handsomely. Illingworth was able to declare at 245 for 3 wickets at the tea interval on the fourth day and there was every prospect of a home victory. India had to bat out time over a period of eight hours to force a draw or score a total of 419 runs to win. By stumps on the fourth day both prospects were very distant. Mankad and Wadekar soon fell and when Sunil was caught behind the wicket off Hutton for 24 India had only one hope remaining —the weather.

The elements did not fail the tourists in their hour of need. With their overnight score standing at 65 for 3 wickets the match was abandoned as a draw shortly after lunch on the final day, without a ball being bowled. There was consensus that India were rather fortunate to still be level at this stage of the series. They could have lost both of the Tests had the weather not intervened but the torrents of rain had done little to assist the Indians in the field. The most marked effect was that the spinners had to operate continually with a wet, greasy ball. For men such as Bedi, Venataraghavan and Chandrasek-har the exercise was futile and, overall, the handicap tended to even the balance between the two sides. The England players were well used to playing in the prevailing conditions, whereas the Indian team were not and it was perhaps appro-priate that the series remained all-square as the last Test approached.

Thus to the Oval and the most monumental day (Monday, 24 August 1971) in the history of Indian cricket. After thirty-nine years of trying and at the twenty-first attempt in England, India finally beat the English on their own territory. Twenty-one was an extremely apt number, for in more ways than one did it signify the coming-of-age of India as a Test nation.

Coupled with their success in the Caribbean, the solitary victory over England four months later effectively made India the world champions of cricket!

In stark contrast to the jubilation and joy of the team triumph, the game for Sunil was a personal failure. Apart from taking two catches during the first England innings his only other distinction was to register his first nought in Test cricket. In the event, the disappointment was short-lived. The victory was all-important and the person who made it possible was Chandrasekhar with his unorthodox, whiplash wrist spin. He ran riot through the England second innings at a time when they appeared to be in total control of the situation.

England had held a marginal lead of 71 runs on the first innings. However, when Chandrasekhar produced his inspired golden spell to take 6 for 38 off 18·1 overs India had an opportunity of victory such as they had never before possessed. England's all-out total of 101 was their lowest-ever against India and with patient, careful batting the tourists showed that the wicket held few terrors. For the loss of 6 wickets the target was duly reached.

In Bombay, 6,000 miles away from London, the traffic came to a standstill as a delirious Indian public celebrated the triumph. By a strange coincidence it was Abid Ali who hit the winning boundary, exactly as he had done in West Indies four months earlier, to record India's first great victory. Now he repeated the exercise and brought to an end England's record run of twenty-six consecutive Test Matches without defeat. Instantly, India were hailed the new world champions although the team still had much to prove before they could justly claim the title.

Sunil could return home feeling more than satisfied with his first tour of England completed. He hit three first-class centuries against various counties and a festival team whilst in the Tests he batted extremely competently, if not indulging in run-sprees of Caribbean vintage. There would be a full year's break from Test cricket now for him before facing England once again. The significant difference was that the next series would be in India which meant, on his eighth appearance for his country, Sunil would finally play a Test Match on his native soil. Long had he waited for that moment to arrive and he could look forward to it with justified pride.

Averages for 1971 series v England, 3 Tests, played 3

Tests	Inns	NO	Runs	HS	Average	
3	6	0	144	57	24·00	*Bowling:* 15–3–42–0
						Fielding: 5 ct

Results: England 0, India 1, 2 Tests drawn

Accumulative record

Tests	Inns	NO	Runs	HS	Average	
7	14	3	918	220	83·45	*Bowling:* 16–3–51–0
						Fielding: 6 ct

4 Muted Progress

Plans were quickly made so that the victorious Indian team would be greeted in a manner befitting their newly acclaimed status of world champions of cricket. The homeward-bound plane was diverted to New Delhi, where the Indian Prime Minister greeted the nation's triumphant sportsmen and in Bombay there was a red-carpet welcome as promised. A motorcade through the streets was only part of the mammoth public reception accorded the players and numerous functions were organised but unfortunately for Sunil he was to miss it all. He had to participate in a double-wicket tournament in Bermuda and consequently missed the celebrations.

'From all accounts', he said, 'the public reaction was one of overwhelming joy.' Such public acclaim by the fanatical Indian supporters is understandably difficult for other followers of cricket to imagine. However, there are few Test players who have actually played in India who will deny the description. The atmosphere on Test Match days at the grounds in Bombay, Calcutta, Kanpur or anywhere else in India defies description. It is an experience the players do not readily forget. A red-hot cauldron, bubbling over with noise of all kinds (human, man-made and, at times, explosive!) is a fair picture of the highly partisan Indian public. In the light of this hero-worship it is not surprising that the players are given superstar status and if the team happens to win the crowd immediately goes wild with delight.

On returning home from Bermuda, another honour was bestowed on Sunil. It was an invitation to play for the Rest of the World on a tour of Australia arranged to replace the originally planned tour Down Under of the South African team. Five unofficial 'Tests' were played and overall Sunil had a moderately successful tour. His highest score was 95 against New South Wales in the second match and in three other innings he reached a half-century. It was Sunil's first experience of facing really fast bowling, in the shape of Dennis Lillee, but by the time he returned to India in February 1972 his education had been extended.

Another debut was looming in sight for Sunil on his return from Australia. Then Ranji Trophy had progressed to the knock-out stage but before Bombay began those games Sunil played for West Zone against East Zone at Jamshedpur in the Duleep Trophy. For two years he had been very disappointed not to be picked for the Zone side but he could afford to have a quiet laugh. His eventual selection had come only after having played for a World XI and to force the point home Sunil underlined the errors of the selectors in not choosing him earlier by scoring a century.

The good form continued in the Ranji Trophy. In the quarter-final against Bihar, Sunil hit the highest score of his career to date, 282, although when taking a catch later in the game he sustained a hair-line fracture of the thumb. There were doubts about his fitness for the Ranji final but after much deliberation he took his place in the Bombay side to play Bengal. Another century, 157, came from Sunil and the result was Bombay's fourteenth successive victory in the Ranji Trophy.

The date was April 1972, the end of the Indian domestic season, which usually begins during the previous September but Sunil's season had begun in September 1970. Through touring commitments and two home seasons he had been playing cricket non-stop for eighteen months. There had to be a rest period, a time when the young player could recharge his batteries and Sunil was more than glad to put away his cricket bag for a few months' relaxation. Then it could come out again in September in readiness for another confrontation with England. This second encounter with the English would be on Indian soil and the impatient Indian fans would be able to see their heroes in Test Match action for the first time in two years. Indian cricket was riding on the crest of a wave but was about to plummet very rapidly back to earth in the opening encounter of the new series. Defeat was the one thought nobody entertained and when it occurred India was rocked.

Preparations for MCC leading up to the First Test at New Delhi were not ideal for an important match. Only three first-class games were played, two against zonal sides who could not offer the type of opposition the tourists needed to put the players in the right frame of mind for the Test. In all probability, the players themselves would have been quite happy to escape from the Test with a draw. That they won was a measure of their professional approach and although it was against the odds, the victory was a great morale-booster, giving an added fillip to an already eagerly awaited series. Not surprisingly, the defeat was a bitter pill for the Indian public to swallow. They, and the team, were badly shaken but Sunil was his usual philosophical self about the unexpected reverse.

'The England team deserved their win', he said, 'because they played better than us. It was in fact a jolt, and a timely one, that we couldn't afford to be complacent.'

Complacency, over-confidence, a very professional England team and a brilliant spell of bowling by Geoff Arnold were the main contributions to the defeat. Arnold took 6 for 45 as India slumped to 173 all out in the first innings, from which

9 Sunil Gavaskar hits out during the first Test against England in 1974.

10 John Edrich stretches to try and cut off the ball.

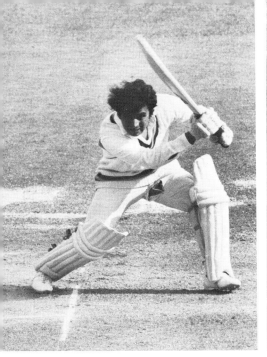

11 & 12 *(above left)* Another boundary for Sunil Gavaskar off the bowling of Mike Hendrick; *(above right)* Abid Ali (*left*) who had himself scored 71 congratulates Sunil Gavaskar on reaching his century at Old Trafford, 1974.

13 *(below)* The Indian fans rush on to the pitch; Mike Denness tries to protect Sunil Gavaskar from being mobbed.

point defeat was always apparent, despite England's having to score 200 plus in their second innings. At 107 for 4 wickets the match hung in the balance but India could capture no more wickets and England won comfortably by 6 wickets to take a very surprising one–nil lead in the Series.

In the match, India's first Test for fifteen months (since beating England at the Oval in August 1971) Sunil continued his succession of low scores. A mere dozen runs in the first innings were followed by even fewer in the second innings, just 8 and it appeared that the flow of runs was receding to a trickle. Indeed, it had, because the two-innings aggregate of 20 runs in the First Test was to be repeated in both the Second and Third Tests. It was a highly unusual hat-trick for a batsman of his class to make 20 and no more in three consecutive Tests!

The scores for each match were 12 and 8; 18 and 2; and 20 and 0 not out, although in the latter two games victory each time more than compensated for the depressing run of low scores Sunil was experiencing. No batsman can continue to score centuries indefinitely and Sunil was no different from anybody else. In the light of future events there is every reason to view this sequence of failures as the inevitable reaction after his initial batting glut in Test cricket. It was perhaps a period of acclimatisation, of ever-growing maturity and experience. At the moment he was in the middle of the period and it would not be until two more years had elapsed that Sunil would become the complete master opening batsman. Until then patience would be needed; the wait would be well worthwhile because the Sunil Gavaskar who completed his Test apprenticeship would prove to be the most successful Indian batsman in history.

The Second Test at Calcutta was a very close-run affair. The margin was just 28 runs in India's favour but, close as the England last-wicket pair took the score to the required target, the Indian team always expected to win.

'On a pitch which turned from the first day there was only

going to be one result, an Indian win,' said Sunil. 'The last wicket troubled us but we were sure we were going to win.'

The important feature of the match was India's first innings total of 210 all out. That was the highest innings of the match! Sunil's confidence obviously depended on the lethal Indian spinners. In the event it was the spinners who won the match for India, taking nineteen of the England wickets to fall. Chandasekhar claimed nine victims, Bedi seven and Prasanna three, with Abid Ali claiming the solitary wicket for the medium-pace bowlers. England were bowled out for 174 in the first innings, a deficit of 36 runs, and India's 155 all out in their second innings left the visitors a target of 192 for victory. When the ninth England wicket fell with 148 runs on the board the game was virtually over but Old and Cottam bravely prolonged the suspense, adding another 25 runs and making the final result appear much closer than it actually was.

At Madras, India won by 4 wickets to take a two–one lead in the series, the result at the end of the fifth Test. This decisive Test began with the unlikely sight of England batting against an opening attack comprising Ekuath Solkar and Sunil Gavaskar! The strategy was not particularly unusual, strange though it may seem. Sunil had already turned his arm over in six of his ten Tests, albeit to no great effect, and in the previous series against England he had sent down twelve overs in the Old Trafford Test, principally because Solkar had been injured. At Madras, his bowling stint lasted precisely one over and the spinners were brought into operation. Chandrasekhar again wreaked havoc, taking 6 for 90, and England struggled continuously while reaching 242 all out.

A first innings lead of 74 runs ensured India victory when England were bowled out again for a paltry 159 runs but the 85 runs required were only reached after 6 wickets had fallen. Sunil did not open the second innings as he had a hairline fracture of the thumb and when he went to the crease, batting at number eight, he had merely to play out one over and let

'Tiger' Pataudi hit the winning runs from the next. Earlier in the innings, the one explosive incident of the series occurred when Wadekar did not walk after an appeal for a catch. The umpire at the bowler's end decided to consult his colleague and in the following few moments the England players came dangerously close to intimidating the officials. Tony Greig gave a perfect illustration of an Apache wardance, Alan Knott flung his gloves into the air and there was a general air of indignant outrage in the atmosphere until skipper Lewis restored sanity. The whole affair was unnecessary for, with so few runs to chase, it was always patently obvious that India were going to win.

Kanpur and Bombay were the venues for the Fourth and Fifth Tests, where drawn games were almost as certain as the Indian victory had been in the Third Test. Not only did India take the series, two games to one, but there was also a return to form by Sunil, although he was still a long way from reproducing the batting displays of 1971. He scored a half-century in each game. This meant he had passed the 50 mark on 11 occasions from 24 Test innings and, if the centuries had disappeared for the time being, there was still a remarkable air of consistency about his batting. Of the two innings, the first at Kanpur was the most significant.

The match was the fourth of the series and Sunil made his highest score, 69, from his total of ten visits to the crease but it was not his 50 that was particularly important. Run 22 was his 1,000th run in Test cricket. Coming in his eleventh Test the milestone had been reached in fewer appearances than by other previous Indian batsmen but statistically the record was a trifle disappointing. His very first series had produced the near-record 774 runs against West Indies in just four Tests. Against that run-spree, it took Sunil another seven more Tests to score the requisite 226 extra runs to reach 1,000 in all. There had to be a moral: perhaps Sunil had simply played too much cricket at the outset of his Test career.

The home series against England came after a break of

more than a year from Test cricket and until the Fourth Test Sunil was clearly out of touch. In fact, he had played ten consecutive Test innings since scoring his last half-century and it was only now that his form began to return to a standard remotely near to his best. In making 67 in the second innings of the second drawn game at Bombay (Fifth Test) the good form remained with him. However, there was no more Test cricket planned for India until mid-1974 and the process of reaching a peak, in terms of consistent batting performances, was to be a long drawn-out affair. Important at this stage was that Sunil was beginning to recapture some of his Test form. It would also continue fifteen months later in England but by no means was Sunil approaching a peak of any description.

It was far too early for greatness to be thrust upon Sunil and there was a real danger that his exploits in West Indies two years earlier would be classed as a fluke if his Test record did not improve. The one point that many critics forgot was that he was still only twenty-three years old when the England series in India was played. Thirty is not an unreasonable age for a batsman to reach full maturity and it appears that too much was expected too soon from Sunil, mainly because of the wonderful debut he had made in Test cricket. In time, the full promise and potential would be revealed but until then patience would be needed.

As for the Fourth and Fifth Tests against England Sunil had no hesitation in saying that there was no chance of definite results. 'The wickets at Kanpur and Bombay were flat and easy-paced so there was no chance of a result unless one side collapsed and batted badly, which did not happen.' Thus, the series went to India and once again the claim went up from millions of supporters that India were world champions: India had now beaten England twice, at home and abroad. Add the West Indies series and India possessed a very fine record in Test cricket between 1971 and 1973 which read: P 13 W 4 D 8 L 1, with three series won in the process.

Sunil was more reticent than his fellow countrymen. 'Since we hadn't played Australia it is not a valid claim.' he said, 'though I feel we had a side that would have beaten Australia then.' Sadly, the theory was not put into practice. India would not meet Australia on Test Match terms until 1977–8, by which time the face of cricket would have changed dramatically, as well as India's own standing among the six cricketing nations of the world. As if to underline how rapidly fortunes can change in cricket, India would then have resumed her former station with perhaps only New Zealand holding less prominence. Without Sunil Gavaskar and Vishwanath to bolster the batting, the situation would have been desperate.

With the Test series finished it was back to the Ranji Trophy for Sunil. Already, between the Second and Third Tests, he had scored 160 against Gujarat in the West Zone league for Bombay and more was to follow in the knock-out stage of the competition. In the quarter-final against Madhya Pradesh, Sunil hit 135 followed by 134 in the semi-final against Hyderabad. No batsman had a hope of making a century in the Final. It was played against Tamil Nadu at Madras on a viciously turning pitch where the highest score from four innings was a meagre 155 all out by Bombay at the first attempt. Nevertheless, Bombay had sufficient bowlers to dismiss Tamil Nadu twice for 66 and 61 runs and thereby win the Trophy by 110 runs for the fifteenth time in succession.

Season 1972–3 had come to a satisfactory conclusion. Sunil's number of first-class centuries was steadily growing, although the following two seasons were rather barren for him. Only two three-figure scores came from his bat. Both were in the annual Irani Cup matches between the Ranji Trophy holders and the Rest of India. As Bombay lost the Ranji Trophy during the 1973–4 season, the second century was made for the Rest team and, with Bombay's surprising loss, a chain of events was set in motion that was to have far-reaching consequences.

Bombay's captain, Ajit Wadekar, came under heavy criticism for the loss of India's premier trophy, although it had no effect on his role as the leader of the national team. Following the 1973–4 home season, India would travel to England for a short three-month tour lasting from April to July. The tour was to be no less than catastrophic for Indian cricket. Everything that could have gone wrong did go wrong and the way the whole affair rankled with the players was summed up precisely in one small comment by Sunil. When asked if the tour was bad from beginning to end his usually phlegmatic approach to cricket and life in general slipped slightly. 'Yes,' he answered, 'it was a tour one should forget in a hurry.'

Average for 1972–3 series v England, 5 Tests, played 5

Tests	Inns	NO	Runs	HS	Average	Bowling: 4–2–7–0
5	10	1	224	69	24·88	Fielding: 2 ct

Results: India 2, England 1, 2 Tests drawn

Accumulative record

Tests	Inns	NO	Runs	HS	Average	Bowling: 20–5–58–0
12	24	4	1,142	220	57·10	Fielding: 8 ct

5   Defeat and Controversy

Losing the Ranji Trophy was only a small part of the steadily accumulating trouble Ajit Wadekar had to face during 1974. The Duleep Trophy and the Irani Cup also went to teams other than Bombay and West Zone by the end of the 1973–4 season. There was pressure for him to face but he had yet to lose a Test series as India's captain so there was no real reason for him not to be selected for the tour of England. In many ways, Wadekar was the unwitting 'fall-guy', or scapegoat, for the shambles that passed as the 1974 Indian tour to England but there was much more to the whole affair than simply the fallibility of the captain.

The main problem was India's position as one of the premier teams in the world. Defeat had to come at some time or other but the defeats meted out by England in the three Tests were so heavy that any challenge from the Indians appeared non-existent. Clearly a captain must accept some responsibility for the manner in which his team performs. With Wadekar the criticism went beyond the normal constraints, particularly at home. Yet it was to Wadekar that Indian owed most for the successes enjoyed by the team during the preceding three years. Of this, Sunil had no doubt and the views of a cricketer who played under Wadekar for Bombay, West Zone and India must be heeded.

'Ajit Wadekar should be given the major credit for our emergence as a major cricketing power,' said Sunil. 'He got the best out of a talented lot of cricketers. In fact, he tapped the hidden potential of a lot of cricketers in the team and got the seniors to contribute. The credit should go solely to him and our fielding, which improved beyond recognition during his captaincy.'

If achieving nothing else, Sunil's comments do help to straighten the record against a much-maligned former captain of India but there was much off the field which contributed to the dramatic slump by the team. However, the ostensible reason was the Test Matches and to give the clearest indication of the train of events they must be dealt with first, followed by the underlying factors which probably played a more significant part in the developing furore. Ironically, despite a defeat, Sunil began the series with his first Test century for over three years, since hitting his fourth hundred against West Indies in 1971.

Old Trafford staged the First Test, where the weather was bitterly cold. With intermittent rain also hampering play, India were kept in the field for the better part of two days while England scored 328 for 9 declared. India replied with 246 all out but, apart from Sunil's score of 101, only Vishwanath, with 40, and Abid Ali, 71, of the remaining batsmen reached double figures. The long awaited fifth Test century from Sunil was his first against England and he followed it with a competent 58 in the second innings. India's victory target was 296 but, apart from Sunil and the ever-dependable Vishwanath, the batting was not strong enough to sustain the chase. The last 5 wickets tumbled for 43 and England were the victors by 113 runs. A comfortable enough victory for England but what was to be gruelling for India was that the margin of defeat at Old Trafford was to be the least bad of the three Test results in the series. And so to Lord's, where the first of two humiliating innings defeats awaited the tourists.

Defeat was always imminent for India after England had amassed a total of 629 all out yet for three days the team fought very hard to stay in the match. On the second day, during the last hour's play, and again the following morning, Sunil and Engineer enjoyed a splendid opening partnership that gave hope of the follow-on being averted. They added 131 runs for the first wicket before Sunil was caught behind for 49. Unfortunately the rest of the team could not match the efforts of the openers except, of course, for the now customary contribution from Vishwanath, who hit another half century. The innings closed at 302 all out and Denness, then England's captain, immediately enforced the follow-on, although there was time for just two more overs on the third day before close of play.

When play resumed on the Monday, the blackest day in Indian cricket history had dawned. The paying customers deserved a refund under the Trades Description Act. In seventy-five minutes India were shot out for 42, their lowest-ever Test score and also the lowest Test score to be recorded at Lord's, and the recriminations were about to begin. In 1952, India had capitulated for a meagre 57 all out in the face of Fred Trueman's record bowling spell, which saw him take 8 for 31. Twenty-two years later the Indian team could not manage to pass the half-century and by no stretch of the imagination did England possess a bowler remotely near the class of Trueman. It was total, dismal capitulation with the scorecard reading as shown overleaf.

Numerous theories were advanced for the pitiful scorecard after the match. Unfortunately, there are few excuses that can be put forward. There was no resistance whatsoever from the batsmen and just as the tour as a whole was best forgotten 'in a hurry', so too with this dismal display. In any event, the fun was only just beginning in terms of retribution for the team and they had enough problems coming from other quarters to worry overmuch about one calamitous performance.

England v India

Second Test 20, 21, 22, 24 & 25 June 1974 at Lords

England	1st Innings	
D. Lloyd	ct Solkar b Prasanna	46
D. L. Amiss	lbw b Prasanna	188
J. H. Edrich	lbw b Bedi	96
M. H. Denness	ct sub b Bedi	118
K. W. R. Fletcher	ct Solkar b Bedi	15
A. W. Grieg	ct & b Abid Ali	106
A. P. E. Knott	ct & b Bedi	26
C.M. Old	b Abid Ali	3
G. G. Arnold	b Bedi	5
D. L. Underwood	ct Solkar b Bedi	9
M. Hendrick	not out	1
Extras b8 lb4 w2 nb2		16
Total		629

Fall of Wickets

1	2	3	4	5	6	7	8	9
116	337	339	369	571	591	604	611	624

Bowling	O	M	R	W
Abid Ali	22	2	79	2
Solkar	6	2	16	0
Madan Lal	30	6	93	0
Bedi	64·2	8	226	6
Chandrasekar	9·3	1	33	0
Prasanna	51	6	166	2

India

	1st Innings		2nd Innings	
S. M. Gavaskar	ct Knott b Old	49	lbw b Arnold	5
F. M. Engineer	ct Denness b Old	86	lbw b Arnold	0
A. L. Wadekar	ct Underwood b Hendrick	18	b Old	3
G. R. Vishwanath	b Underwood	52	ct Knott b Arnold	5
E. D. Solkar	ct Underwood b Hendrick	43	not out	18
B. P. Patel	ct Fletcher b Grieg	1	ct Knott b Arnold	1
S. Abid Ali	ct Arnold b Old	14	ct Knott b Old	3
S. Madan Lal	ct Knott b Old	0	ct Hendrick b Old	2
E. A. S. Prasanna	ct Denness b Hendrick	0	b Old	5
B. S. Bedi	b Arnold	14	b Old	0
B. S. Chandrasekhar	not out	2	absent hurt	0
Extras	b4 lb7 nb12	23	Extras	0
	Total	302	Total	42

Bowling	O	M	R	W	O	M	R	W
Arnold	24·5	6	81	1	8	1	19	4
Old	21	6	67	4	8	3	21	5
Hendrick	18	4	46	3	1	0	2	0
Grieg	21	4	63	1	—	—	—	—
Underwood	15	10	18	1	—	—	—	—
Lloyd	2	0	4	0	—	—	—	—

Fall of Wickets

1st Innings

1	2	3	4	5	6	7	8	9
131	149	183	188	250	280	281	286	286

2nd Innings

1	2	3	4	5	6	7	8	9
2	5	12	14	25	28	30	42	42

England won by an innings and 285 runs

The series concluded at Birmingham with another innings thrashing for the Indians to complete a thoroughly miserable four months in England. For Sunil the summer ended disastrously too. He made 0 and 4 in two innings in the Third Test and the 'duck', the second of his career to date, was made the more unpalatable because he was dismissed off the very first ball he received. That was another notable 'first' for his career statistics but a feat Sunil would not be keen to repeat often in the future. In the match, England won easily by an innings and 78 runs. to comprehensively beat India three–nil and the prospects were that the players would receive a hostile welcome when they returned home. Before they left England, the Indian team had heard disquieting reports of the ugly mood the fans were showing in public but fortunately their anger was not directed physically towards the team when they arrived back. There ended an inglorious chapter in Indian cricket history and the pertinent question is how or why did the tour fall apart as it did, to be played out in such a lack-lustre spirit?

There is no one answer to that perplexing question. From the point of view of the captaincy it is probable that long before the tour was completed the burden of the appointment had become too much for Wadekar. However, the reverses against England were the first experienced by India since he had assumed the mantle of leader in 1971. Wadekar's overall record was outstanding, far better than any previous Indian captain, but the bitterness of defeat tended to blind disappointed supporters. What those highly critical supporters did not see was the mounting tension that crept through the team off the field. To a large extent Wadekar had to shoulder the responsibility for the débâcle on the field but external factors played a major role in dictating how much of the poor play and ill-feeling that caused it came openly to the surface. At times the external influences far outweighed the simple business of playing cricket and consequently the tour began to disintegrate.

Two incidents of the many that occurred well away from a cricket field give the perfect example of how unsavoury the tour became. Although both occurred almost simultaneously they were entirely unconnected. In the first affair, an unholy argument broke out because it was alleged that the team had insulted the Indian High Commissioner.

On the day after the Oval Test (of infamous 42-all-out fame) the players had been invited to attend a party at the High Commissioner's residence. The appointed time for arrival was 6.30 pm but before that the players were also due to attend a function at the State Bank of India's London office from 5.45 pm to 6.15 pm. There was an unavoidable delay (explained the following day when incident number two came to light) on leaving for the bank function and as a result the team did not arrive until 6 pm. Once there, the players were confronted by several London-based Indian journalists who wanted to know how the team had come to be bowled out for 42 the day before. Not content with the answers, the journalists proceeded to accuse the team of arguing amongst themselves, spending too much time drinking and other general misdemeanours. Not a few of the players defended themselves vigorously, letting the journalists know their opinions in no uncertain terms. Sadly, this served only to make the journalists intent on some form of revenge and the perfect vehicle for it was only minutes away: the High Commissioner's party.

The team eventually arrived at the party at 7 pm and because of parking problems the players had to walk up the driveway to the residence. Sunil, in company with Vishwanath, was amongst the last to walk towards the house but by the time they reached the porch they met Ajit Wadekar coming *out* of the house, looking very grim indeed.

'He has told us to get out,' was Wadekar's crestfallen reply to questions – 'he' being the High Commissioner.

The team returned to their coach where noisy consultations began. Lt Col H. R. Adhikari pleaded, cajoled and finally ordered his team to return to the party. The senior players could see no point in going back. The host had said 'get out', which was rather explicit, while others felt that the captain had been insulted. Finally, it was Venkataraghavan who urged they join the party. They did, but by then the damage had been done.

Once inside, very few of the players accepted the snacks available, although they were not discourteous as most accepted a drink. However, that was all the ammunition the Indian journalists required. Reports immediately began circulating, publicly and privately, that the Indian High Commissioner had been snubbed and insulted by the cricketers. Twice they were late and for that they deserved a ticking-off but there the matter should have ended. It did not and the attack on the team even named individual players. Bishen Bedi was a target for allegedly making uncomplimentary remarks while, in reality, what he actually said was exactly right about an affair which received too much bad publicity.

'If we had won, even if we had turned up late, there would have been no problem,' said Bedi, 'but, just because we've lost we get the stick.' How perceptive those words were!

On the day following the diplomatic discord another bombshell exploded: one of their number had been accused of shoplifting and that was the reason for the team's late departure for the function the previous evening. The manager had been engaged in urgent consultations with various authorities at exactly the same time as the team was preparing to depart for the first function. Also, the absence from both of the functions of the player in question was immediately explained. His name is not important. The manner in which the case was handled was and, again, the tour party was shrouded with bad publicity.

In essence, the player concerned was advised to plead guilty and the matter would be kept out of the newspapers and, therefore, quickly forgotten. What occurred was quite bizarre. The player was accused of stealing two pairs of socks, which were discovered underneath a pair of trousers which he had paid for. Moreover, only minutes earlier he had also paid for *twenty* pairs of socks (he was shopping for other members of the team as well as for himself) and in that lies the crux of the matter. It is very doubtful that a man will pay for twenty pairs of socks and then deliberately attempt to avoid payment for a miserable *two* pairs. Be that as it may, the department store management were intent on pressing charges which, inadvisably, were admitted in the haste to get the matter over and done with quickly. The unfortunate player should have been allowed to take his defence as far as possible, if needs be in front of a judge and jury.

It is common knowledge that magistrates rarely, if ever, dismiss charges when a defendant pleads not guilty. The reputation of the police is such that they appear to take the view that a policeman is incapable of lying and in this case it is highly likely that the same pattern would have emerged concerning the security officers of the store. Consequently, the only course of action was for the player to elect for trial by jury and in view of the facts the possibility of an acquittal must have been very high. As it was, another black mark went against the touring party and by the time the final match of the tour was completed the players must have been heartily sick of the sight of England.

So much for England. Whether India would be any better was doubtful and the players had every reason to feel nothing but dejection as they returned home.

Averages for 1974 series v England, 3 Tests, played 3

Tests	Inns	NO	Runs	HS	Average	Bowling: 1–0–5–0
3	6	0	217	101	36·16	Fielding: 1 ct

Results: England 3, India 0

Accumulative record

Tests	Inns	NO	Runs	HS	Average	Bowling: 21–5–63–0
15	30	4	1,359	220	52·26	Fielding: 9 ct

6 End of a Captain

Many questions were awaiting answers as the 1974–5 season approached. West Indies were scheduled to play a five-Test series in India and the whole structure of the Indian team was in danger of being scrapped in the wake of the performances in England. One event in particular showed the vehemently hostile feelings that the supporters were capable of displaying. There had been the usual post mortems, with the main criticism being directed at Ajit Wadekar but at Indore the people went much further than merely throwing mud at players.

A concrete bat had been erected at Indore to commemorate India's famous 1971 victory over England and on the top was inscribed Ajit Wadekar's autograph. The monument was defaced with tar and other substances and the crowds even went so far as to stage a demonstration at the house of Wadekar's mother. 'Generally', said Sunil, 'a cricketer was not good news.'

Little attention appeared to be paid to logical reasoning at the time of these demonstrations. India had played three consecutive Test series against the same team, England, a fact which had to have some bearing on the eventual results. 'The

14 The end of a fine innings: Sunil Gavaskar is run out for 101 during India's first innings at Old Trafford in 1974.

15 Dennis Amiss is caught by Sunil Gavaskar, having scored 47 in the first Test, 1974.

16 *(above)* Tony Greig takes evasive action as Sunil Gavaskar cuts a ball from Derek Underwood to reach his 50 in the second innings at Old Trafford.

17 *(left)* Mike Hendrick is driven for 4 during the last day's play in the first Test, 1974.

Englishmen got used to our spinners,' Sunil pointed out with some justification, 'particularly Chandra, and this helped them no end.' Another point not easily recognised by the people in India was that in 1974 their team encountered some atrocious weather conditions totally alien to the tourists. 'We like the sun on our backs to perform well', said Sunil, and of that commodity there was precious little during the summer of 1974. Apart from the weather, it was accepted that England were the superior side in the series but as the defeats had been so heavy it appeared inevitable that heads would roll when the West Indies series began.

On an administrative level there are seldom changes made when the team loses. That left only the players to carry the full weight of defeat. 'A lot of the team were on the chopping block because of their performances', said Sunil, 'but eventually there were few new faces when we played West Indies.' While that comment was perfectly true it was somewhat ironical following the bitterness, hurtful suggestions and hostile reception meted out to the players either during or after the tour of England—but such is Indian cricket. At times, it is a total enigma, as can be illustrated by the one major change that did occur in the Indian team for the visit of West Indies. This was Ajit Wadekar's retirement from first-class cricket. There are many misconceptions on this subject and, although Wadekar had experienced a lean time as India's captain, he was certainly *not* stripped of the captaincy but retired in the very early weeks of the 1974–5 season.

Sunil was on his honeymoon at the time Wadekar announced he was packing his bags. To Sunil, the decision came as a great surprise. He thought Wadekar still had four years' cricket at least left in him but the decision was swift and irrevocable. It came after Wadekar was dropped from the West Zone side after a Duleep Trophy game at the start of the season. For an Indian captain to be dropped from a zonal team was unthinkable. To have lost the captaincy may have been bearable (and understandable after Wadekar's record over the previous twelve months at home and abroad) but he should not have been dropped from the zonal side altogether. Consequently, Wadekar decided to retire instantly from the first-class game. The zonal team question was the real reason for his decision, not any pressure from other administrative quarters as was said at the time, and by it India lost not only a loyal player but their most successful captain in over forty years of Test cricket.

Who would take over the leadership? To some people the final choice was a little surprising, 'Tiger' Pataudi being recalled to lead the national side after an absence of almost five years from Test Match captaincy, although he had made three appearances against England during the 1972–3 home series after showing splendid form against the tourists in a representative match. Sunil must have had an outside chance of the captaincy because he was made Pataudi's second-in-command for the West Indies series but age was the probable deciding factor, Sunil being under twenty-six when the Tests began. In any event, he was quite satisfied to be vice-captain, fully endorsing the choice of the selectors.

'He was the only person with the necessary experience and qualifications to rebuild the morale of the shattered side', said Sunil of Pataudi, 'and he did a superb job although personally he had a poor series.' Commenting further on Pataudi's influence Sunil added. 'If he had batted with his usual flair I think we would have won the series, which we lost 3–2.'

Modesty obviously forbade Sunil from adding another significant point. Not only was Pataudi's brilliant, dashing strokeplay not in great evidence during the Tests but Sunil himself was missing from three of the games and the loss of two leading batsmen, either through poor form or injury, was a heavy burden for the rest of the team to carry. Sunil played in the First Test, making a modest 14 followed by his third Test nought in the second innings, and was then unavailable until the Fifth Test three months later. Three was the operative number, that being the number of times he broke his right index finger during the 1974–5 season and it was not until the New Year that it finally healed correctly. It was a depressing time on the sidelines for Sunil, made all the worse because the original injury robbed him of the opportunity to lead his country for the first time.

In the First Test, which West Indies won comfortably by 267 runs, Pataudi had also broken a finger when taking a fine running catch in the tourists' second innings. Until this stage of the game there was nothing to choose between the sides. West Indies, batting first, had scored 289 all out, to which India replied with 260 all out but at the second time of asking the visitors were able to declare at 356 for 6 wickets. This set India a target of 386 runs to win at a run a minute but without both Pataudi and Engineer the batting collapsed to 118 all out to give West Indies a one–nil lead in the series. An extra disappointment for Sunil was his nought in the second innings. 'Even as a mere substitute skipper it was terrible that I should begin with a duck.'

The chance to make amends was not far away. Pataudi was unfit for the Second Test and Sunil was appointed captain in his place. The news stunned and delighted Sunil: 'I was in a severe daze', he said, but before the Test there was a Ranji Trophy match to be played against Maharashtra and on the first day came the sickening bone-crunching sound of ball against hand as Sunil faced Salgaonkar, the opposition's opening bowler. There began three months of sheer frustration for Sunil. Playing in the Second Test was out of the question and the chance to lead his country had gone.

Pataudi returned for the Third Test but not Sunil. At Calcutta, in the nets he discovered he could not hold the bat in comfort, let alone play any shots, and had no alternative but to stand down from the side. The finger improved and Sunil made the journey to Madras for the Fourth Test, where he began with fielding practice. There was no apparent trouble with the finger but on the following day when batting in the nets against Karsan Ghavri it was struck again. The result was inevitable. It was broken again and Sunil missed his third Test of the series. Finally, the finger healed in time for him to resume in the Fifth Test at Bombay, by which time the series stood at two–all. The scoreline represented a remarkable fight-back by India, who had lost the first two Tests and bounced straight back to win the Third and Fourth. In keeping with the current practice the last game was extended to six days as the series was still open.

Greater interest than usual was stimulated in the Fifth Test, with it being the first international fixture to be played at the newly-built Wankhede Stadium. The new venue had been built in amazingly quick time and was named after the Vice-President of the Indian Board of Control, Mr S. K. Wankhede. A victory would have made a fitting opening at the ground but West Indies had other plans, winning easily by 201 runs. They batted first, totalling 604 for 6 declared, with a double century from Lloyd and a century from Fredericks boosting the score. Prior to the Test Sunil had not played any first-class cricket for nearly two months and he had reservations about playing but his first innings effort quickly dispelled any doubts.

The innings began badly with Engineer falling without scoring but Solkar stood firm with Sunil to add 168 runs for the second wicket. With a mere five minutes' play remaining on the third day Sunil fell to off-spinner Gibbs for 86, a delightful innings spiced with numerous fine forcing strokes against the pace of Roberts. It was a timely return to form for Sunil, after missing most of the series through injury.

The runs had begun to flow from his bat again and the score was significant in that it marked the definite beginning of a new era, or phase, in his Test career. In the second innings he made only 8 when India were set to score 404 runs for victory. The target was never a possibility and West Indies won by 201 runs to take the series 3–2, the first occasion that a five-Test series in India had produced a definite result in every match. The series was lost but India had fought magnificently after being 2–0 down. After the trials and tribulations of recent months the outlook was much brighter for Indian cricket. 'At least the morale was good', said Sunil, 'and people forgot our dismal tour of England.' Yes, that was all now firmly in the past and everybody could look forward to the future, none more so than Sunil.

Averages for 1974–5 series v West Indies, 5 Tests, played 2

Tests	Inns	NO	Runs	HS	Average	Bowling:
2	4	0	108	86	27·00	Fielding: 1 ct

Results: India 2, West Indies 3
Accumulative record

Tests	Inns	NO	Runs	HS	Average	Bowling: 21–5–63–0
17	34	4	1,467	220	48·90	Fielding: 10 ct

The completion of the West Indies series at the end of January 1975 is an ideal stopping-off place to review what Sunil had accomplished in terms of performances past and performances still to come. The careers of many leading players tend, inevitably, to fall into sections. With Sunil this was particularly true and the 1974–5 series marked the end of phase one in his career. To date, his achievements had been largely confined to his first Test series in 1971. Magnificently though he had performed then, the follow-up had been no more than moderate.

After seventeen Test appearances, Sunil had gathered marginally less than 1,500 runs. Those had come mainly from five centuries and eight other scores of fifty or more. However, four centuries and three fifties had accrued in his first four Tests, which brought a total aggregate of 774 runs. This meant that in the following thirteen Tests Sunil had scored fewer runs than in the first four. The difference is most notable when comparing the number of substantial scores (i.e. fifty or more) he made in the later Tests. There was a solitary century and five half-centuries. Without doubt the record was still very good but by the same token Sunil had not maintained the form of his first explosive efforts. Indeed, it would have been miraculous if he had.

Four years had now elapsed since Sunil's Test debut. It was long enough to form the basis of a sound apprenticeship. What he now had to do was carry forward the good work and 'come into his own'. After the West Indies series he would have another full year's break from the international game, a feature which had been evident already on several occasions in his short career. After winning in England in 1971, India had not played another Test Match for fifteen months. Similarly, after beating England at home during 1972–3 a Test Match break of sixteen months had followed, before playing England again. The added fact that it was the same opposition time after time was also not the most stimulating formula to bring out the best in players. Staleness can easily creep into a player's game and this could have happened with Sunil. Finally came the injury-ridden series against West Indies, in which Sunil had little opportunity to make an impact.

All in all, progress had of necessity been stuttering rather than in leaps and bounds. Significantly, when India resumed Test cricket in January 1976, there were four separate series scheduled between then and the following February (1977). It was a far cry from the 'now and then' basis India had been playing under from 1971 to 1975. The difference in Sunil's play was that all the promise and potential he had shown would knit together and produce the record-breaking batsman in full flight that had been threatening the world's bowlers for so long without actually achieving ultimate success.

Before the accolades of 1976 descended upon Sunil there was a certain amount of trouble on a closer horizon awaiting India's premier batsman. First, there was a disappointing loss of form in the Ranji Trophy matches as the 1974–5 season drew to a close following the series against West Indies. For the second successive season Sunil failed to hit a century in the Ranji Trophy, although Bombay did avenge the defeat of 1973–4 by Karnataka and regain the chapionship. His single three-figure innings of each season came in each of the annual Irani Cup matches, raising his personal total of first-class centuries to twenty-two. The thrice-broken finger was a considerable handicap during the 1974–5 but, in similar circumstances to those of his Test career, Sunil was to remedy the matter at the start of the next season. Before that could begin there was another trip to England imminent and this would bring his second, more serious, problem.

The inaugural Prudential World Cup Tournament was to take place in England during two weeks in June 1975. Against one-day specialists such as England and West Indies, there was no serious possibility of India winning the competition. Undaunted, the team took its rightful place in the tournament under the captaincy of Venkataraghavan but in the opening match Sunil became involved in one of the most puzzling incidents of his whole career.

The game was against England, who rattled the scoreboard along at such a rate that they scored 334 for 4 wickets in the allotted 60 overs. Victory was out of the question for India but their final score of 132 for 3 wickets was a very poor reflection on the efforts of their batsman after 60 overs at the crease. To make matters worse, Sunil's score was 36 not out! He had stayed throughout the innings and the howls of protest that reverberated around the cricket grounds of England were long and loud. Nor were they confined to England, as Sunil would discover later. He described the innings as being 'by far the worst I have ever played' and towards the end he was simply going through the motions of batting. It was as if a mental block was stifling completely his whole cricketing nature. The only way to curtail the agony was to get out. That was even harder than batting—he was dropped three times off simple chances. The position became unbearable for him. He felt like moving away from the stumps as the bowler delivered the ball, thereby giving away his wicket. It was a curious position; Sunil could not force the pace but neither could he get out and at the end of the day it was plain for all to see that he would be the subject of a searching inquiry.

The manager, Mr G. S. Ramchand, was apparently satisfied with Sunil's explanation. 'I have never been a player who could force the pace', he said, 'and England's attack was too professional to have a wild slog.' There the matter ended in England but once back in India Sunil received a letter from the President of the Board of Control asking for an explanation of the England affairs because it appeared that the manager had reported Sunil for playing slow cricket. Furthermore, the report went on to suggest that Sunil persisted in playing slowly and that had a demoralising effect on younger members of the side as well as being against India's best interests. In his own words, Sunil was 'on the mat'.

The outcome of the enquiry was odd. The Board censured Sunil for batting slowly, telling him that his explanation was not satisfactory but the proceedings would be terminated at that point. In effect, the Board gave Sunil the benefit of the doubt. As they were not likely to dismiss out of hand one of the two top batsmen in the country there was little else the Board could do. Nonetheless, the 'verdict' was inconclusive, and certainly did nothing to foster good relations between players and the Board of Control.

'All this left a very bad taste in the mouth and did precious little to spur our players to do better in future', he said, but a far more illuminating comment came when he spoke of limited-over cricket in general, which caused the rift originally. 'It neither enthuses me nor embarrasses me', he said.

7 The Climb to the Top

Sunil's major task as the 1975-6 season approached was to put behind him the unhappiness of the World Cup fiasco and the disappointment of missing three Tests the previous year. Broad new horizons beckoned him, beginning with what amounted to a world tour early in 1976. The tour began with a three-Test series in New Zealand, followed by a return visit to the West Indies. The Kiwis were new Test opposition to Sunil, while the happy memories of his first visit to the Caribbean were sufficient to make him as eager as the proverbial beaver to make the four-month cricketing pilgrimage.

The players would be more than pleased to return to India after their lengthy period away from home and not merely for reasons of homesickness. At times, the cricket would be more akin to war, particularly in the West Indies, but on a personal level the two series were of crucial importance to Sunil's career. During the four months abroad he re-emerged as a world-class opening batsman and at the end of the twin tour was firmly on course for yet another Indian batting record. His performances at Test level may have been somewhat muted in the preceding series but with the dawning of 1976 a rejuvenated Sunil set about the bowlers of the world with a vigour that had been long awaited. With the runs flowing freely again, records once more began to fall to his bat and when 1976 drew to a close Sunil's second career phase had produced a rich seam of highly consistent run-scoring.

In preparation for the forthcoming tour, Sunil signified his return to form with three splendid displays in the Ranji Trophy when the 1975–6 home season commenced in October. Successive centuries of 112, 190 and 171 against Gujarat, Maharashtra and Saurashtra were a great morale-booster to Sunil's erstwhile sagging spirits and for good measure he slammed 203 off the touring Sri Lanka attack in an unofficial four-day Test at Hyderabad. The added responsibility of being Bombay's newly-elected captain appeared to have no effect on his play. It was quite the opposite, and Sunil's famed concentration was more intense than ever before as he settled down to his new position with spirited determination. The West Zone league games of the Ranji Trophy had progressed very satisfactorily. If the same could hold true when India's party departed for New Zealand the prospects were very bright indeed for both India and Sunil personally.

Immediately prior to the announcement of the officials for the touring party Bishen Bedi, the exquisite left-arm spinner, was hauled before an enquiry committee to explain certain remarks he had made to officials of the Vidarbha Cricket Association. Evidently the remarks were justified, for the mercurial bowler was named captain of the touring team. Although appearing in front of a tribunal is far from funny, the sequel did have its lighter side. 'Bishen must hold the record for the number of enquiries he had to face,' said Sunil, and he too was not totally unaccustomed to the procedure. Consequently, they made a good pair when Sunil was announced as vice-captain and, to make the party complete, P. R. 'Polly' Umrigar was chosen as manager. The redoubtable Polly had had his fair share of entanglements with authority in his playing days. In racing parlance there was only a short-head and a neck between the three when deciding who was the most forthright and, unlikely as it was, the threesome appeared to be a good composite mixture for the strenuous tour ahead.

Two first-class games preceded the First Test against the Kiwis and the Indians won both comfortably. Central Districts were beaten by 6 wickets and Northern Districts by 141 runs, but Sunil was taking some time to adjust to the new country. His scores were 0, 2, 30 and 2. It was not the most inspiring start to the tour but during the latter game Bishen Bedi pulled a muscle during fielding practice and the accident gave Sunil the ideal spur. Bedi was ruled out of the Test due to start two days later and Sunil achieved another ambition by captaining his country for the first time.

Auckland was the venue. Losing the toss was an initial disappointment but words of wisdom from his former captain Ajit Wadekar reminded Sunil that all was not lost; 'I never mind if I lose the toss, so long as I win the Test', were Wadekar's sentiments and they proved to be prophetic for the young man following in his footsteps. The first day progressed quite well for India. Under their new leader, the bowlers performed more than adequately to dismiss the Kiwis for 266 with a few minutes remaining for play. Two overs were all that time allowed when Sunil, in company with Dilip Vengsarkar, began the reply. Sixteen were on the board without loss at close of play but on the second morning Vengsarkar went in the first over.

Sunil was joined by Surinder Amanath, elder brother of Mohinder, and together they ensured that India would gain a substantial first innings lead. They had some good fortune, both being dropped three times but they capitalised handsomely to add 204 runs for the second wicket. The partnership lasted four hours twenty minutes and, notwithstanding their good luck, both played numerous fine attacking shots. Surprisingly, for somebody making his Test debut, Amanath was the dominant partner, racing to 124 before falling to Hadlee. In scoring a century, Surinder emulated his father, the well-remembered Lala Amanath who had also scored a hundred on his Test debut against England in 1933–4. It was a remarkable double for a remarkable cricketing family.

Sunil, if slightly outpaced, was not to be outdone. He soldiered on with customary caution to duly register his sixth Test century, which was also a double 'first' in that it was his first against the Kiwis in his maiden Test against them. 'I had to really struggle to get the runs,' said Sunil, which underlined his earlier poor form on the tour but it was a splendid beginning to the Test year and augured well for the next eleven months.

The eventual lead stretched to 148 runs, the Indian first innings ending on the third day at 414 all out. The wicket was beginning to turn and Prasanna was soon in his bowling element. Wicket after wicket fell to him. In all, he claimed 8 for 76, his best Test figures and with New Zealand bowled out for 215 India's victory target was a mere 68.

Sunil once more was in the forefront of proceedings scoring 35 not out to lead his team in perfect fashion to a splendid 8-wicket victory. 'It was exhilarating to win my first Test as captain', he said of the win, adding characteristically, 'The team work was tremendous and it was indeed most satisfying'.

The result at Auckland was well merited for a number of reasons. The team had batted, bowled and fielded with distinction but the greatest handicap they had to face was the umpires. Appeals were constantly turned down. Leg before wicket or bat–pad catches all received the same negative treatment and early in the game Prasanna said philosophically, 'Well, we've got to bowl them out'. Bowl them out the Indians did, but a measure of their exasperation was made clear towards the end of the match when Chandrasekhar bowled Wadsworth to conclude New Zealand's second innings. He performed a war dance appealing for the wicket to which the umpire retorted by saying 'He is bowled'. Chandrasekhar, quick as a flash, said, 'I know he is bowled, but is he out.' The remark was a classic cricketing comment as well as giving

Indian views on the standard of umpiring in New Zealand.

Repartee could readily fall from Sunil's lips too. The intervening match between the First and Second Tests was played at Dunedin against Otago. 'Dunedin is very *near* the South Pole,' he said, 'but the weather made us feel as if we were *on* the South Pole.' The game was drawn, washed out by rain, and the party made for Christchurch, where the Second Test was to be played. Bedi returned to the side as captain but bad weather seriously interfered with the game. A draw became inevitable and at the end less than three innings were completed.

Sunil fell to Collinge early in the Indian first innings for 22 and only Vishwanath, 83, and Mohinder Amanath, 45, made significant contributions to the total of 270 all out. In reply, the New Zealanders batted very slowly. Despite the inclement weather they could have been well placed at the end of the first innings. A lead of 133 runs was more than useful but, with the loss of time adding to the very long New Zealand innings, India experienced little trouble in batting out time for a draw. Once certain of ensuring New Zealand would have to bat a second time the game ceased to be a contest. Sunil made 71 in the second innings, maintaining his fine form in the Tests but the outstanding performance in the match came from wicketkeeper Syed Kirmani. In the one New Zealand innings he claimed six victims, five caught and one stumped, to equal the then world record for the number of dismissals in an innings by a wicketkeeper, although it has since been beaten by Pakistan's Wasim Bari and again by England's Bob Taylor.

The Third and final Test of the series began at Wellington on 13 February, a month after the tour began. From victory, to a draw, to a comprehensive defeat was to be the disappointing progression for the Indians with the conclusion of the Wellington match. New Zealand won by an innings and 33 runs to gain their first-ever Test victory by such a margin. It was a poor conclusion to the series but worse still was the injury Sunil received during the New Zealand innings.

India had batted first, totalling 270 all out and as New Zealand scored 403 all out Sunil was hit a sickening blow in the face from a fiercely pulled shot from Lance Cairns. The result was a fractured cheekbone but it could have been much more serious. Cairns puts a lot of power into his strokes and Sunil was only a few yards from the bat when the ball was hit. He had made 22 in the first innings but now there was no opportunity to improve on that—he was out of action for the rest of the match. Thus New Zealand levelled the series at one–all but at least India's record of never having lost a Test rubber to the Kiwis had remained intact. Next, it was the West Indies again.

In an exact repeat of 1971 Sunil was seriously injured as he was about to make the journey to the Caribbean. Then his finger had caused the problem, now it was a fractured cheekbone and the injury required three weeks' rest before he could resume cricket. Some of the recuperation period was spent sightseeing in New York but all too soon the demands of a cricket tour overrode such diversions and Sunil made his way to the West Indies. The first part of the twin tour had passed with a fair degree of success for India and Sunil. The weather and the umpires had been the main stumbling blocks but events in the West Indies were soon to make it appear like a picnic in comparison to the latter part of the exercise.

On a personal basis, apart from the injury, Sunil was in excellent form. His Test average was back above 50, after falling below for the first time at the end of the 1974–5 West Indies series and now he was returning to the scene of his greatest triumphs. More landmarks were in sight. The aggregate of 266 runs made against New Zealand pushed Sunil's total Test aggregate very close to 2,000 runs in all. In Indian cricket that target was a notable distinction. When it was reached Sunil would be among the top ten highest-scoring Indian batsmen in history, with only Vishwanath of present-day players for company. With his sixth full Test series completed, and the seventh rapidly approaching, all manner of records were becoming available to him, both in the near and rather more distant future. They would come, but first there was the small matter of a Test series against the West Indies to be played; and that was to be one of the most bitterly fought cricket campaigns of all time.

Averages for 1976 series v New Zealand, 3 Tests, played 3

Tests	Inns	NO	Runs	HS	Average	Bowling:
3	5	1	266	116	66·50	Fielding: 5 ct

Results: New Zealand 1, India 1, 1 Test drawn

Accumulative record

Tests	Inns	NO	Runs	HS	Average	Bowling: 21–5–63–0
20	39	5	1,733	220	50·97	Fielding: 15 ct

8   Scenes of Former Glory

Sunil's second Caribbean visit again entailed four Test matches because as the First Test did not start until 10 March there was not time to play the normal five games. With the enforced rest keeping Sunil out of the team until his injury had fully healed, there was time for him to play only one first-class game before the First Test. This was against Barbados, who inflicted a very heavy 10-wicket defeat on the Indians, the third successive occasion they had lost to the Island on a Caribbean tour. Sunil showed in the first innings that his confidence had not been affected by the bad blow received in New Zealand. The psychological damage could have taken much longer to put right than the physical discomfort but a confident innings of 62 dispelled any fears.

The Kensington Oval at Bridgetown appeared to be a perfect batting pitch when Bedi won the toss and decided to bat. Sunil, batting with a new partner Parthasarathy Sharma, initially justified the decision, putting on 51 runs for the first wicket. With his score at 37, Sunil went lbw to Roberts from a ball that kept low and from that point onwards the innings fell apart. The dismissal was disappointing. Sunil had been batting very soundly, with Roberts receiving severe punish-

18 Tony Greig watches as a leg-side delivery is punished. The third Test, at Madras, 1977.

19 The fifth and final Test at Bombay in England's 1976/7 tour of India. Sunil Gavaskar drives Peter Lever for 4 runs.

ment to any deliveries that erred in length. The Barbadian got an early revenge and it was one of the rare occasions when Sunil was dismissed when in the thirties in a Test Match. Usually, when he got that far the scene was set for a half-century at least. After 63 Test Matches, encompassing 119 innings, his scores between 30 and 39 numbered a mere four. Clearly, once the 30 mark was reached, it was a danger signal to any bowling side.

The Indian first innings of the Bridgetown Test was completed before tea on the first day with 177 runs the meagre total. West Indies proceeded to prove that there was no real venom in the wicket by stroking 488 for 9 declared, with centuries from Lloyd and Richards. The total was more than adequate for the task before the home bowlers. India could muster only 214 runs in the second innings, to lose their second consecutive Test by a margin greater than an innings, the final difference being an innings and 97 runs. Sunil scored a solitary single in the second innings before succumbing to a short-pitched delivery from Roberts. He mistimed the hook, was caught at short-leg and a most inauspicious return to West Indies was completed.

One small consolation was the venue for the Second Test. It was Port of Spain's Queen's Park Oval, scene of Sunil's Test debut five years earlier and one of his favourite grounds. His previous two Test innings there had produced centuries and this occasion was to be no exception, his third consecutive three-figure performance being a record for the ground. He could not bat until the third day of the game. Rain prevented any play at all on the first day and Bedi took a calculated gamble in asking West Indies to bat first when he won the toss. Richards slammed a pulsating century but there was scant assistance from his compatriots and early on the third day Bedi's decision had proved correct with West Indies all out for 241.

A good base to the innings was imperative for India's victory hopes. It did not materialise. Vengsarkar went for nought and the Amanath brothers and Vishwanath also lost their wickets when barely into double figures. Thus, shortly after tea on the third day, India stood at 126 for 4 wickets with only Sunil standing firm against the West Indies pace attack. Brijesh Patel was his next partner and it was now vital that they stayed together; the loss of another wicket would have been disastrous. India could rest secure; not only did the pair remain but added 204 runs for the fifth wicket in a partnership stretching into the fourth day. At the end of the third day Sunil had reached 90. With the aid of several sharp singles the century was duly achieved, the seventh of his Test career and second in two months.

The partnership flourished until Sunil reached 156 and the score was 330 for 4 wickets. Holding made one delivery deviate a fraction off the pitch and Sunil's eight-hour occupation of the crease was over. The fifth-wicket stand was an Indian record against any country. Also, the marathon innings was the highest Sunil had played since scoring a double century on the same ground in 1971. The increasing authority in his batting was well evident in this performance, giving extra weight to the opinion that Sunil had returned emphatically to peak form. The disappointments and frustrations that culminated with the season of the thrice-broken finger were in the past. Centuries were again becoming Sunil's staple Test diet and the early months of 1976 were the turning of the tide in terms of his Test career.

As for the progress of the Second Test, Patel also went on to record his maiden Test century before Bedi declared at 402 for 5 wickets with a lead of 161 runs. Time was against a definite result but India could conceivably have won on the last day if all the chances offered by the West Indian batsmen had been accepted. They were not and a draw became a formality. It was on the last day that a sense of acrimony crept into proceedings for the first time in the series. It was the first of several incidents totally against the normal code of accepted conduct in a Test Match. The flashpoint would come in the Fourth and final Test at Kingston when all hell broke loose around the Indian batsman. The 'Richards incident' may have had some bearing on future hostilities but in the Second Test Bedi was quite within his rights as the laws of the game applied at that time.

The incident began on the morning of the last day. Richards, during the previous day, had been off the field with a leg strain but was able to bat when the time arose. However, he slipped and fell, aggravating the injury and asked Bedi if he could retire. Bedi intimated that Richards could have a runner but, if he wanted to he could retire, with Bedi exercising his right to state when Richards could bat again. Richards was not in favour. The umpires were consulted and Lloyd, the West Indies captain, also appeared on the field to try to sort out the problem. It was a decision by Bedi that quite obviously upset Lloyd. Richards eventually retired but neither he nor his captain were happy and after tea the point was forcibly made to Sunil by Lloyd himself.

Lloyd was batting when play resumed after tea and as Sunil walked on to the pitch he jokingly said to Lloyd: 'When is the declaration coming?' As West Indies were barely level with India at the time the question was hardly serious but Lloyd was not in a jocular mood. 'You want me to declare when your captain won't let my batsman retire!' The sporting spirit was beginning to depart from the series with that complaint from Lloyd.

After the draw at Port of Spain, the Third Test was scheduled for Georgetown. Days of continual rain made the exercise futile and to prevent the Test being washed out, the venue was changed to Port of Spain. Nobody would be more delighted to be going back to Trinidad than Sunil! His lowest Test score there was 65 and he had every intention of keeping the record intact. He did not, but the lapse was only a temporary first-innings aberration. The second innings was more than adequate compensation and the final result of the Third Test rivalled any of India's past Test achievements.

Indeed, in many ways, the eventual victory at Trinidad surpassed all that had gone before: India's maiden victories on West Indian and English soil in 1971 had been very special but the Third Test was no less historic.

The barest details of the match show that India won by 6 wickets. What was remarkable was the total they achieved to make victory possible, 406 for 4 wickets. In scoring over 400 runs to win the fourth innings of a Test Match India became only the second team in Test Match history to perform the feat. The first had been Bradman's Australians at Headingley in 1948 and India's repeat performance placed the side in élite company. The triumph was a real team effort throughout the game, especially as West Indies appeared to have a stranglehold on the match after each side had batted once. India's fight-back was amazing, justly earning the right to go in the record books for magnificent all-round performance.

West Indies batted first, the innings's central figure being Richards who slashed the bowling to all parts of the ground for 177 runs. The all-out total was 359, to which India replied with 228 all out. Sunil fell lbw to Holding for 26 to record his lowest score at Queen's Park Oval and began to wonder if his succession of big scores on the ground had run their course. It was to be hoped they had not, for when West Indies batted again they were able to declare at 271 for 6 wickets after lunch on the fourth day. At that stage, the last thought to enter Sunil's mind was of victory. 403 runs were required, with the alternative of batting a day and a half to save the game but, despite the magnitude of both tasks, Sunil was confident that the side could achieve a draw. The wicket was still playing well and they had the added bonus of a decent first-wicket partnership when the second innings began.

Batting with Anshuman Gaekwad, his third opening partner in as many Tests, Sunil helped to take the score along to 69 before losing the tall, elegant right-hander from Baroda. Mohinder Amanath strode to the crease and with excellent application was still there at close of play on the fourth day.

94

He was batting so well that Sunil was supremely confident that India could force a draw. The score stood at 134 for 1 wicket with Sunil undefeated on 86. On the last day, made up of six hours' playing time, India required a further 269 runs to win.

Initially, progress was slow on the final morning. Sunil took over an hour to gather together the 14 runs he required for his eighth Test century (and fourth at Port of Spain) but as the main thought was survival, not a run chase, the situation was not desperate. Sunil was unable to move back into top gear but it was not for the want of encouragement by the spectators. A calypso had been composed in recognition of his heroic deeds in 1971 and the song was audible to him throughout the innings, as if willing him to reach three figures.

> *It was Gavaskar*
> *The real master*
> *Just like a wall*
> *We couldn't out Gavaskar at all*
> *Not at all*
> *You know the West Indies couldn't*
> *Out Gavaskar at all.*

(From a calypso composed by Lord Relator in honour of the visiting Indian cricket team to the West Indies in 1971.)

The melody to the verse was catchy but after hearing it throughout his innings Sunil was tired of it, even though it had the desired effect! The joy of the crowd was shortlived after the long-awaited century was reached. Sunil added just two more runs before he was caught behind, to make the score 177 for 2 wickets. With victory still a non-existent notion, Sunil was disappointed. He thought he had let the side down but his replacement, Vishwanath, had other ideas. Perhaps he was aided slightly by Lloyd's decision not to take the new ball when it was due. The spinners stayed on and when the speed merchants did return Vishwanath was firmly in the batting groove, but from the imperious manner in which he despatched Holding's bouncers to the fence it would not have made a great deal of difference. The run-rate increased dramatically with the new ball and suddenly, when the tea interval arrived, a stupendous victory was a definite possibility for the Indians.

All the while, Mohinder Amanath had remained impassive, playing the sheet-anchor role to perfection. He remained, while others (Sunil and Vishwanath) scored the bulk of the runs and he was still there after tea when Vishwanath reached his century. The third-wicket partnership ended after adding 159 runs, when a misunderstanding resulted in Vishwanath being run out, which was the only way he looked like being dismissed, and when the final 20 overs began 65 runs were the easily accessible target. Brijesh Patel made certain, hitting boldly to score 49 not out and the goal was achieved in the eleventh over. Mohinder was run out for 85 at 392 for 4, just 11 runs short of the target, an unfortunate loss when so close to victory. He, as much as anyone, had ensured victory but overall it was a marvellous team effort by all concerned. Sunil's hundred gave the start, Mohinder was the rock, Vishwanath the strike-force and Brijesh Patel's sprightly knock was the icing on the cake. By any standards, it was a truly great performance.

A humorous aside from the famous Third Test triumph came when Sunil related the story of a spectator he had first met in 1971 when playing at Queen's Park Oval. Then, the spectator had wagered $100 to $1 that Malcolm Foster would not score a century when he was batting in the Second Test. At the time the wager was struck Foster was on 99! And he was bowled without adding to his score! Sunil paid the man one dollar. Five years later he met the same man who struck another 100–1 bet that India would score the 402 runs for victory. Such is the way Trinidadians enjoy their cricket, 'in a typically crazy way', said Sunil. It cost him another dollar in 1976 but he cared little and it was with true feeling that he could say, 'That's Trinidad for you. Trinidad, I love you!'

The full scorecard of India's historic win at Port of Spain is shown on pages 98 and 99.

Amidst the happiness of victory it was almost possible for Sunil to miss another important milestone he had passed during the game. The forty-seventh run of his century innings was his 2,000th in Test cricket, coming in his twenty-third Test appearance. The first thousand had taken eleven Tests, thus Sunil was maintaining his 'average' rate of scoring. Nearing twenty-seven years of age and his best years as a batsman ahead, there were surely more milestones awaiting him in the future.

From calypsos, joy and glory in Trinidad the series both climaxed and plummeted to outright cricket war with the Fourth Test. Sunil called the match 'Barbarism at Kingston', while another apt description would be the Battle of Kingston. Both phrases were not an exaggeration. The game caused a storm of protest and West Indies 10-wicket victory was hollow in the extreme. They beat only half a side because the other half had been hospitalised by the intimidatory direct-attack methods used by the bowlers.

The match began with a surprising decision when Lloyd asked India to bat after winning the toss. The wicket was expected to favour the fast bowlers and it was very bouncy during the first morning's play. Undaunted, Sunil and Gaekwad advanced the score to 60 without loss at lunch. It was after the interval that the West Indies bowling tactics became immediately apparent. Holding began bowling around the wicket and straightaway loosed three bouncers at Gaekwad. Sunil's turn for the same treatment came shortly afterwards. Four bouncers and a beamer were his share from one over alone, with Holding pretending the beamer accidentally slipped from his hand. The 'accident' happened again in the next over and Sunil then knew that there was a deliberate ploy afoot to intimidate him and Gaekwad.

Lloyd evidently did nothing to curb Holding from aiming

West Indies v India

Third Test 7, 8, 10, 11 & 12 April 1976 at Port of Spain

West Indies

Batsman	1st Innings		2nd Innings	
R. C. Fredericks	ct Amanath b Chandrasekhar	27	ct Solkar b Chandrasekhar	25
L. G. Rowe	ct Vishwanath b Chandrasekhar	18	ct Kirmani b Venkataraghavan	27
I. V. A. Richards	ct Chandrasekhar b Bedi	177	ct Solkar b Venkataraghavan	23
A. I. Kallicharran	b Chandrasekhar	0	not out	103
C. H. Lloyd	ct Gaekwad b Chandrasekhar	68	ct Vishwanath b Chandrasekhar	36
D. L. Murray	b Chandrasekhar	11	ct Solkar b Bedi	25
B. D. Julien	ct Vishwanath b Bedi	47	ct Kirmani b Venkataraghavan	6
M. A. Holding	lbw b Bedi	1	not out	17
Imtiaz Ali	not out	1		
A. L. Padmore	ct Gavaskar b Bedi	0		
R. R. Jumadeen	lbw b Chandrasekhar	0		
Extras	lb7 nb2	9	b2 lb7	9
Total		359	(for 6 wkts declared)	271

Fall of Wickets

1	2	3	4	5	6	7	8	9
45	50	52	176	228	334	357	358	358
41	78	81	162	214	231			

Bowling

Bowler	O	M	R	W	O	M	R	W
Madan Lal	6	1	22	0	11	2	14	0
Amanath	5	0	26	0	11	3	19	0
Solkar	9	2	40	0	—	—	—	—
Bedi	30	11	73	4	25	3	76	1
Chandrasekhar	32·2	8	120	6	27	5	88	2
Venkataraghavan	27	7	69	0	30·3	5	65	3

India

	1st Innings		2nd Innings	
S. M. Gavaskar	lbw b Holding	26	ct Murray b Jumadeen	102
A. D. Gaekwad	ct Murray b Julien	6	ct Kallicharran b Jumadeen	28
M. Amarnath	st Murray b Padmore	25	run out	85
G. R. Vishwanath	b Imtiaz	41	run out	112
E. D. Solkar	b Holding	13		
B. P. Patel	ct Fredericks b Holding	29	not out	49
S. Madan Lal	ct Richards b Holding	42	not out	1
S. Venkataraghavan	b Imtiaz	13		
S. M. H. Kirmani	lbw b Holding	12		
B. S. Bedi	b Holding	0		
B. S. Chandrasekhar	not out	0		
Extras	b11 lb6 w4	21	b10 lb12 w1 nb6	29
	Total	228	Total (for 4 wickets)	402

Fall of Wickets

1	2	3	4	5	6	7	8	9
22	50	86	112	147	182	203	225	227
69	177	336	392					

Bowling	O	M	R	W	O	M	R	W
Julien	13	4	35	1	13	2	52	0
Holding	26·4	3	65	6	21	1	82	0
Lloyd	1	0	1	0	6	1	22	0
Padmore	29	11	36	1	47	10	98	0
Imtiaz Ali	17	7	37	2	17	3	52	0
Jumadeen	16	7	33	0	41	10	70	2
Fredericks	—	—	—	—	2	1	1	0

India in won by 6 wickets

at the batsman while the crowd positively bayed for him to continue. Repeated shrieks of 'Kill him, man', or 'Hit him, man', as Holding bowled left no doubt as to their feelings. After facing such a barrage it was not surprising afterwards that Sunil wrote: 'All this proved beyond a shadow of doubt that these people still belonged to the jungles and forests, instead of a civilised country.' Harsh words, but entirely justified when the intention of the bowlers was solely to hit the batsman. Despite the bumper barrage the first-wicket stand reached 136 before Sunil was yorked for 66 and by close of play the scoreboard showed India at 178 for 1. Only sixty-seven overs were bowled all day, of which the last thirty were predominantly short-pitched.

On the second day the situation deteriorated rapidly. Lloyd claimed the new ball and Holding was on the offensive with bumper after bumper. Mohinder Amanath went first, deflecting a ball while trying to keep his head in contact with his shoulders. A similar ball greeted Vishwanath and a short while later he too fended away a delivery with his knuckles that left a finger both fractured and dislocated. However, as his hand was in front of his face at the moment of impact that was infinitely more desirable than the alternative. Shortly before lunch a batsman was, inevitably hit on the head. Gaekwad, who had already suffered numerous blows on the arms and body, was hit behind the left ear. He had to retire but what made the incident far worse was the reaction of the crowd. Sickeningly, they clapped and cheered. Little wonder Sunil passed such a low opinion on them.

In the pavilion the situation was no better. Nobody was interested in Gaekwad. The team manager 'Polly' Umrigar was already at the hospital with Vishwanath and the Jamaican cricket officials appeared unconcerned. Only when Sunil intervened and insisted on some action was Gaekwad taken to hospital and within minutes he was joined there by a third casualty. Brijesh Patel stopped a bouncer with his mouth and, with the score at 306 for 6 wickets, Bedi decided enough was enough. He declared, not because India were well placed but to save his remaining batsmen (i.e. the bowlers) from injury.

Worse was to follow when India took the field. Bedi, attempting a fiercely struck caught-and-bowled chance aggravated a finger injury and Chandrasekhar did exactly the same, only with the worse result of fracturing his thumb. The position became so acute that all seventeen members of the touring party had to field at one time or another during the West Indian first innings. On the last day, twelfth man Surinder Amanath was rushed to hospital with appendicitis and that final straw completely filled India's cup of woe. Eventually, West Indies were bowled out for 391, 85 runs ahead, but the problem for India was in finding enough batsmen fit enough to hold a bat.

The task was impossible. Five players were injured and the Indian second innings terminated at 97 for 5 wickets. It was not a declaration; Bedi had no choice but to record the innings as completed simply because he had no fit players left to bat when the fifth wicket fell. Consequently, West Indies required just 13 runs for one of the most disreputable victories ever achieved in Test cricket.

The tour had ended sourly. There were press conferences, accusations and counter accusations and the whole affair was a sad reflection on Test cricket. The suggestion that Indian batsmen could not play fast bowling was ludicrous. Sunil and Vishwanath were world-renowned batsmen and they and others did not shirk at the prospect of facing fast bowling: 'Fast bowling is the West Indies' strength and it was always on the cards that the bumper would be bowled frequently,' said Sunil.

The Indian batsmen knew what kind of reception they were likely to receive and they accepted the bumper as a fair tactic. When asked if he agreed with this Sunil replied, 'Yes, but having said that I think it can be overdone.' During the Kingston Test it was overdone to the point of lunacy. How a bowler can run up to the wicket time and time again with

101

the sole intention of hitting the batsman is beyond comprehension. Yet Sunil had no doubt that the West Indian bowlers had that express desire. When asked the point-blank question, 'Were the bowlers aiming deliberately at the batsmen?' Sunil answered unequivocally, 'Yes, in the Kingston Test, in the first innings.' That is a sad condemnation of a wonderfully talented cricket team who had no need to resort to such tactics. They could win by virtue of their many other talents without stooping so low. On their day, West Indian cricketers in full cry are the finest sight in the world of cricket: batsmen, bowlers and fielders alike. The Kingston Test of 1976 against India tarnished the image but if the lessons to be learnt were heeded it should never happen again.

On the brighter side, Sunil had much to enthuse about as he flew home to India. His first-born son was awaiting his arrival in Bombay, the happy event occurring when he was in New Zealand, and he was to be named Rohan, after West Indian star Rohan Kanhai. On the cricket scene, the picture was also very rosy. The long-term tour had produced 656 Test runs from seven appearances and another record was hovering tantalisingly on the horizon. New Zealand and England were due to tour India later in the year and by December 1976 Sunil would have four more Tests to his credit. With well over 600 runs to his name there was now a distinct possibility that Sunil could become the first Indian player to score 1,000 runs in a calendar year. There was a three-Test series against New Zealand to play, plus the first of five against England before the end of December. The target was within touching distance and the law of averages augured well for the chase. The seven Tests completed by the end of the Caribbean tour gave Sunil an average of 59·65 per innings. With a possible eight innings remaining in the year an average of 43 was required. If Sunil maintained his present average, it would be a formality, but events never progress as easily as that. Would he do it? As the New Zealand series began all India was asking that question but

Sunil would keep everybody guessing until the last possible moment. In an exciting, tense run-chase of a much different nature from normal Test Match conditions it was to be very very close-run affair.

Averages for 1976 series v West Indies, 4 Tests, played 4

Tests	Inns	NO	Runs	HS	Average	Bowling:
4	7	0	390	156	55·71	Fielding: 2 ct

Results: West Indies 2, India 1, 1 Test drawn

Accumulative record

Tests	Inns	NO	Runs	HS	Average	Bowling: 21–5–63–0
24	46	5	2,123	220	51·78	Fielding: 17 ct

9   Pursuit of a Record

New Zealand's reciprocal visit to India began in November 1976, after a similar visit to Pakistan during the preceding two months. Three Tests were scheduled and following a short, much-needed close-season break on returning home from the Caribbean, the year was becoming progressively more hectic for Sunil. An added, unseen factor was the gradual build-up of pressure for him to bat well. All India wanted to see him reach 1,000 Test runs before the end of the year. With some luck, and not a little skill, Sunil would achieve the distinction and in October, playing for West Zone against South Zone, a brilliant innings of 228 showed that he had lost none of his form. Surprisingly, it was only his second century in the Duleep Trophy, but it was sufficient to serve as a warning to nearby Kiwis that he was determined to make a bold effort for the 1,000-run record.

There was an ironical touch to the First Test, played at Bombay during the second week of November. Although, after twenty-four Test appearances, Sunil was acknowledged as India's premier batsman he had never played a major Test innings at home. To some extent his opportunities had been limited. Seventeen of his appearances had been abroad, which accounts for the high proportion of his aggregate of 2,123 Test runs to date being scored overseas. The balance was 1,791 runs against 332 runs scored at home and he was still waiting to register his first Test century in India. Eight had been scored abroad, whilst at home 86 was Sunil's highest score against West Indies in 1975. The time had arrived for the First Test and Sunil's home city was the ideal place to put the record straight.

India batted first after Bedi had won the toss. The innings was given a sound base with an opening partnership of 120 runs between Sunil and Gaekwad and Mohinder Amanath carried on the good work with Sunil when his first partner went for 42. There was some criticism of the scoring-rate, but a very leisurely over-rate by the New Zealand bowlers did not help the situation. In any event, the first innings of a five-day Test Match needs a solid foundation and that is precisely what Sunil, assisted by Gaekwad and Amanath, gave his side. As a bonus he scored 119, his fourth Test century of the current year. The scoreboard showed 218 for 3 wickets when he eventually fell to the spin of Petherick on the second day and his dismissal signalled a mid-order collapse of quite dramatic proportions. The score advanced a negligible 44 runs while 5 more wickets fell at which point wicketkeeper Syed Kirmani stopped the procession of batsmen to the pavilion. With Bedi, 36, he added 105 runs for the ninth wicket and 42 runs for the last wicket with Chandrasekhar, who made 20 not out. Kirmani was last out for a spirited 88, which raised India's final total to 399 all out.

The New Zealand reply followed a similar pattern. From a relatively strong position of 228 for 4 wickets the innings crumbled to 298 all out, the 101-run lead giving India a distinct advantage. The one facet of the game in their favour was the time element. Consequently, Sunil had to attempt to force the pace in the second innings and he made only 14 before giving Burgess a catch off the bowling of Hadlee. It made no overall difference to the result, and whatever criticisms had been levelled at the batsmen on the first day could not be repeated at the second time of asking. Brijesh Patel scored freely, making 82, and India were able to declare with a lead of 303 runs after thirty minutes play on the last day. This left the bowlers fractionally less than five and a half hours in which to bowl out New Zealand for a second time.

Sunil stepped forward to take up another important role to aid his side towards a well-fought victory when India took the field. He safely held two catches as New Zealand slumped to 27 for 4 wickets and from that calamitous start the Kiwis never recovered. Seven wickets were down for 67 runs and with two and a half hours remaining for play time had ceased to be an enemy. Lees did lead a brief revival, hitting 42 runs but the issue was never really in doubt. The spin of Bedi and company was too much for the New Zealanders and the tenth wicket capitulated at 141, for India to claim the victor's laurels by 162 runs. The spinners claimed 18 of the 20 wickets to fall and with Sunil's significant contribution of 133 runs, plus two catches, together with Patel's second-innings 82, the match was a conclusive team effort by the Indian side.

Despite the fine performance by the team as a whole, 1976 was becoming Sunil's year. The aggregate had risen to 789 runs with four Tests or eight possible innings remaining. The ultimate aim was becoming more apparent with each successive visit to the crease. In the Second Test at Kanpur Sunil did little wrong again, although not scoring as highly as in the Bombay game. Nevertheless, another 81 runs were scored from two innings and the unrelenting march continued towards the '1,000', apparently unabated.

In a match where India completely outplayed the opposition from start to finish a draw was poor reflection on the true course of events. India began by compiling 524 for 9 wickets declared in the first innings. Sunil scored 66, his nineteenth half-century in Tests. No centuries were scored in the innings, a somewhat surprising feature of a very high total which raised hopes that India might have been able to enforce the

20 Sunil Gavaskar pulls a ball from Derek Underwood during his fine innings of 108 at Bombay, 1977.

21 The second Test against Pakistan in Lahore, 1978.

follow-on. Mainly because of a century by Howarth it was not possible, as New Zealand batted into the fourth day to reach 350 all out. Stoppages for bad light also hampered India's push for victory. Bedi was unable to declare until the end of the fourth day, when Vishwanath completed a century off the last ball, because the New Zealand second innings would not have started in the prevailing light. The target for the Kiwis was 383 runs.

When New Zealand lost their seventh wicket at 134, two hours' playing time remained on the last day. With a full day at their disposal the Indian spinners had again bowled exceedingly well and with the time remaining the last three wickets should have been a formality. To the great surprise of all concerned the Kiwi tail-enders put up such dogged resistance that not one more wicket was gained by the bowlers. Lees and O'Sullivan remained resolutely at the crease and at close of play India had to be content with a draw. It was a disappointing finale to a match the home team should have won convincingly.

In India's second innings run-chase Sunil had scored a modest 15. The aggregate had risen to 870 runs for the year and with four possible innings remaining, the record was surely waiting for Sunil to grasp it, but the second-innings lapse at Kanpur was ominous. In his normal form the 130 runs would present few problems to him but a slight tremor was appearing in his usually phlegmatic, nerveless nature and when the series concluded at Madras the record was still very much in question.

India gained an excellent 216-run victory at Madras. The problem for Sunil was that the runs were not flowing from his bat as he would have wished and in the Indian first innings they barely began to trickle. Cairns bowled him for 2! Brother-in-law Vishwanath rectified the situation with an innings of 87 but the all-out total of 298 did not give India any great advantage. However, with their ever-dangerous spinners in prime form, New Zealand had scant opportunity to approach anywhere near a first-innings lead. The Kiwis were dismissed for 140 and when batting a second time India were able to declare with a very large surplus of runs. Bedi set the opposition a target of 360 to win and after their first-innings débâcle New Zealand had very little hope. Bedi himself was the chief architect, claiming 4 for 22 (and 9 for 70 in the match) as New Zealand were dismissed for 143 runs and India clinched the series with a resounding victory.

When building up their big lead, the Indian second innings was noticeable for two features. The first concerned New Zealand pace bowler Richard Hadlee, who became so enraged when an appeal for hit wicket was turned down that he hurled a bail at the umpire. It was a petulant, childish display, not only foolish but stupid in a foreign country. Indian crowds are not renowned for their patience or good humour and in a country where the notice 'Riot Stops Play' is almost as common as the English announcement 'Rain Stops Play', Hadlee could well have had cause to rue his indiscretion later in the day. More important than ill-temper was Sunil's second-innings display. He scored 43, not a particularly large number of runs but considerably more than in the first innings. Moreover, the immediate task in hand was more important than personal records at that particular moment. India required quick runs to enable Bedi to declare and Sunil complied with the instructions from his captain as his mode of dismissal proved. He was stumped, attempting a big hit and, remarkably, that was the first occasion he had been so dismissed in fifty-two Test innings.

With the series against New Zealand completed, Sunil's aggregate had risen to 915 runs. England were already in India preparing for their five-Test series but there was only the first of those games in which Sunil could score the 85 runs he still required. The '1,000' was still very much a possibility, but it was certainly proving to be more than a little difficult to achieve. One creditable aspect of the Kiwi series was Sunil's first Test century in India but, in many

110

ways, it only served to increase the intense pressure that he already was facing as people willed him onwards towards the target.

Sunil explained how certain aspects of playing under pressure affect Indian batsmen in particular by saying, 'To a certain extent, the crowd "plays" with you in India. Therefore, to score runs in India is perhaps far more difficult for Indian players than elsewhere.'

On the personal point of his own impending record, the pressure on Sunil was even greater than for his team-mates. 'With almost everybody willing me to score 1,000 runs in the year, the pressure was intense because after every innings one realised that, in fact, there were not many left. However, the number one priority was always to give the side a good start.'

Averages for 1976 series v New Zealand, 3 Tests, played 3

Tests	Inns	NO	Runs	HS	Average	Bowling:
3	6	0	259	119	43·16	Fielding: 3 ct

Results: India 2, New Zealand 0, 1 Test drawn

Accumulative record

Tests	Inns	NO	Runs	HS	Average	Bowling: 21–5–63–0
27	52	5	2,382	220	50·68	Fielding: 20 ct

10   The Record Achieved

Sunil's twelve-month quest came to an end in December of 1976—it had to because there was but one Test in that month, the first of five against England. The place was New Delhi and if Sunil could not go through to his record in the homely surroundings of Bombay, the capital of India was the next-best substitute. Not that the record was a formality. The 85 runs required would have to be fought for against a powerful touring attack and with England batting first the impatient crowd would also have to wait some time before Sunil made his last-ditch effort to reach the 1,000. Nor too would the waiting be over with the first innings. Sunil fell short of the goal and the drama was carried through all the way. Would he, or would he not? It was totally impossible for the incessantly clamouring Indian crowds to await the answer with bated breath but, like all good fairy stories, Sunil provided a happy ending to the story.

India began the First Test with more success than the eventual result signified. On the first morning England lost 4 wickets for 65 runs and with the wicket taking spin from a very early stage of the match, Indian hopes rose. Amiss, batting for eight and an half hours, gradually wore away India's advantage. His innings of 179 was the central point of England's challenge and, with a first innings total of 381 all out, defeat appeared to be a remote possibility. When India were bowled out for only 122 runs in their first innings, the issue was settled. Sunil was top scorer with 37 in the first of his final two innings of the year. That was 48 fewer than the 85 runs he required and, with defeat staring India in the face, the only remaining interest in the match focused on whether or not he would score the runs in the second innings.

It was impossible for Sunil to escape from the pressure heaped on him because of the impending record. India's second innings began on the third day and at close of play, he was 40 not out. Just 7 more runs required but the next day was the rest day. It seemed that the waiting would never end! Or that the fans would never leave him in peace!

'I was well aware of my 1,000 Test runs because I was just 7 short of the mark when the rest day came and the entire rest day was spent with well-wishers reminding me to score those runs. It was difficult to forget.'

Seemingly unperturbed, Sunil recommenced the task on the fourth day in exactly the same unflappable manner as had characterised so many other Test innings throughout his career. The game barely lasted into the final day and that it was prolonged for so long was due entirely to the skill and technique Sunil demonstrated. He had an enthralling duel with England's Underwood as he led India's resistance. Underwood eventually won that particular game but Sunil had given a batting demonstration of the highest calibre which yielded 71 runs. It was far from being his highest Test innings and it did not save India from defeat, but to Sunil went the final accolade. The '1,000' had been reached.

Yet another record achieved, another milestone passed, must be the brief assessment of the events of 21 December 1976 for the batsman from Bombay. He had travelled a long way, in time, distance and standard of performance, since those early days of cricket in the gallery with his mother.

113

The painful broken nose she had once suffered was worth the discomfort now! Sunil's total for 1976 amounted to an aggregate of 1,024 Test runs, the first time a player from India, New Zealand or Pakistan had achieved the distinction in a single calendar year. At the age of twenty-seven Sunil's claim to world stature was irrefutable. After his brilliant start to Test cricket in 1971 there had been some wavering. Doubts about his ability there were not, but the form had not been consistent enough to proclaim Sunil world-class.

The three missed Tests against West Indies had not aided the situation when he was returning to his best form at the beginning of the 1974–5 season. Nevertheless, class will tell in the final reckoning and that is precisely what happened with Sunil on his return to the Indian team. Following the West Indies series that ended in January 1975, there was a break of a whole year from the rigours of Test cricket before embarking on the twin tour at the beginning of 1976. The benefits Sunil derived from the rest period were his fruitful plunder of runs during the eleven Tests he played that year. He resumed his Test career (and India's Test Match itinerary, for there were no Tests at all in the intervening period) with a renewed vigour that was a delight to watch. For a bonus, he set a record as well. Amazingly, that record was to bear a striking similarity to the events of 1971, surrounding his entry into Test cricket.

As in 1971, when success was a yardstick only to be used in gauging future performances, so it was in 1976, against the background of 1,000 runs in a calendar year. When Sunil opened his Test account with two half-centuries against West Indies, he showed later in the same series that it was a mere starter. The flood-gates did not break open—they were washed away in a three-match torrent of four centuries. A similar event was to occur with regard to his outstanding performance in 1976. Two years later he would not stop at scoring 1,000 Test runs in a single year: Sunil would do it in *seventy-six* days. What was performed once simply became a

114

stepping-stone to even greater deeds and there appeared to be no limits to the heights Sunil could scale in quest of runs. If there were any, they were so far in the future as to be impossible to distinguish. For him, the sky did appear to be the limit.

India had begun the England series with a devastating innings defeat. Sunil's unparalleled achievement was the only bright feature to lighten the gloom and as the series progressed into the New Year, even his outstanding consistency faltered. He could not make a century every time he went to the crease, but if he did not make a substantial contribution to an innings one of India's main problems, their batting strength or weakness, was immediately brought to the fore. Throughout the 1970s India's ability to make a substantial total in any Test Match depended largely upon two players, Sunil and his brother-in-law Gundappa Vishwanath. Both could compare with the best batsmen from any country in the world. They both deserved and earned their place amongst the top rank, but if either or both should fail India's position invariably became critical.

There was a parallel between this aspect of Indian's Test team and the New Zealand side of the 1950s which boasted the very gifted batsman Bert Sutcliffe. He was one of the few truly international-class cricketers that New Zealand produced (J. R. Reid was another) and it has been generally acknowledged that the difference between the Kiwis' drawing or losing a Test Match at that time usually depended upon Sutcliffe being in the side. If he was, a draw was a reasonable expectation, if not, the cause was virtually lost before the contest began. The same was not exactly true of India, because of their world-renowned spin bowlers, but Sunil and Vishwanath were very big fish in a very small batting pool.

Sunil himself always steadfastly maintained a philosophical stoicism about a peculiar problem which has been a feature of Indian cricket for many years. 'The team', he said, 'never seem to play to their full potential.' There lies the key. It is not that the Indian cricketers lack ability; it is more a puzzling mixture of enthusiasm, commitment, and confidence. To say 'We can do it' even if defeated is surely a much more positive attitude to adopt than sighing before a Test Match, 'Oh, well, we might do it.'

Defeat followed defeat with the continuation of the series against England, who took an unassailable three–nil lead by the end of the Third Test. The defeats, bad enough in them-selves, were not the main cause for concern in the Indian hierarchy, it was the manner in which England almost casually brushed aside India's challenge. The first reverse was by an innings, the second by 10 wickets and the third by 200 runs. All too predictably, India's poor performances at New Delhi, Calcutta and Madras were directly linked to the loss of form of their two premier run-makers, Sunil and Vishwanath. In the four completed innings of the Second and Third Test the Indian total did not once exceed 200 and only one batsman, Brijesh Patel, succeeded in scoring a half-century, scoring 56 in the second innings of the Second Test.

Sunil's supercharged run-spree of 1976 could not continue indefinitely. All batsmen have a period of low scores at some stage of their career, often more than once, and Sunil struck such a patch after the First Test. He made 0, 18, 39 and 24 in four innings in the following two Tests and 4 in the first innings of the Fourth Test. Therefore, it was not until the second innings of the Fourth Test, at Bangalore, that Sunil returned to a standard near his known best.

It was during the Bangalore Test that India began the process of redemption, winning by 140 runs and, although the series was already lost, the result provided a much-needed boost to the sagging morale of the Indian team. India batted first, totalling 253, and at first sight it appeared that Sunil's bad form was continuing. He made but 4 and following his nought in the Second Test there was a familiar pattern emerging about these two digits. They were, in fact, the two scores on which he was dismissed the most times throughout his career. For some

116

inexplicable reason, he was dismissed no less than seven times on both scores and the fact did not escape his attention as was discovered when the point was put to him one evening. Chatting one night in a Leeds hotel about this book during the 1979 World Cup, he noticed the scoring chart which appears in the statistics section. When the number 4 was pointed out to him he smiled ruefully and answered, 'Yes, that number does seem to crop up a few times, doesn't it?' It did not worry him and indeed why should it when, in the same statistical sense he could also continue to get dismissed three times on 116! There are a goodly number of Test batsmen who would gladly suffer double the number of ducks and 4s that Sunil scored if they could have a final Test record half as good as his. It is the centuries that count, not the noughts, and Sunil made more than enough hundreds for the failures to be pushed into the background.

India clinched a first-innings lead at Bangalore by dismissing England for 195, quite the most remarkable aspect of the innings being the amazing catching ability of Yajuvindra Singh at short-leg. Playing in his first Test he took five catches, plus two more in the second innings and thereby equalled the long-standing record of catches taken by an outfielder held by Australia's Victor Richardson. Yajuvindra was apparently the successor to India's previous outstanding short-leg fieldsman, Eknath Solkar who was probably the best in the world at the time he was playing. For in only twenty-seven tests, he swooped like an eagle on to its prey to snap up an amazing 53 catches. Surprisingly, despite his record-equalling first appearance, Yajuvindra played only three more Tests between then and the end of the 1979 tour of England, when he finally claimed more regular selection. To some extent, that was Sunil's good fortune, because it enabled him to edge closer and closer to Solkar's catching record. If Yajuvindra had been a regular member of the side he undoubtedly would also have made rapid inroads towards the record total from his high-percentage catch area at short-leg.

Instead, at the end of the 1979 England tour Sunil had more than 40 catches to his credit while Yajuvindra had only 11.

To emphasise their worth to the Indian team, Sunil and Vishwanath batted immaculately in the second innings. On a rapidly deteriorating pitch, both displayed extreme technical application to score half-centuries. Once again Sunil's judgement was perfect against the well-flighted ball with exquisite use of nimble footwork, particularly against his old adversary Underwood. Sunil's score of 50 was passed by Vishwanath's 79 and while being well satisfied with his own performance Sunil was not slow to applaud the innings by his brother-in-law.

'The innings of 50 in the Fourth Test was technically the best because Underwood was making the ball "talk" ' said Sunil, 'but Vishwanath played an even more remarkable innings and his 79 not out was a real gem. In spite of the enormous spin and bounce Underwood got, Vish repeatedly hit him through mid-wicket and was hardly ever beaten.'

By virtue of those two solid contributions India were able to declare at 259 for 9 wickets, setting England a target of 318 runs to win and when their innings began Amiss and Brearley were confronted by S. M. Gavaskar, opening bowler not opening batsman. The spell was brief: just two maidens before Bedi took up the attack and with Ghavri striking to dismiss Amiss for nought at the opposite end India began to take control. When three more England batsmen were dismissed for a paltry 8 runs the grip strengthened to a stranglehold. On the last day Knott alone was defiant but he could not stave off the inevitable. Bedi was the chief tormentor and had it not been for Knott's forceful 81 not out his final figures of 21–34–71–6 would have been more impressive. The victory, India's sole success in the series was well earned, proving that with a little more of the same fighting spirit there were few reasons why the team could not return to the former glory of the 1971–3 era. 'If only' were the two small words at the heart of the problem but theory and practice were poles

118

apart. Nevertheless, the signs for the future were a little better after a succession of defeats.

Once back on the winning trail India had no intention of allowing England any more victories and while the Fifth Test did not produce a result it was the best game of the whole series. The same applied to Sunil, who, after returning to form at Bangalore, was determined to put on a good performance for his own Bombay crowd. The fans were not to be disappointed. India batted first, scoring 338 all out, with the solid foundation of the innings being laid by Sunil. A patiently grafted innings produced 108 runs for his personal total while half-century partnerships were shared with Gaekwad and Surinder Amanath. At 122 for 3 Sunil became the more silent partner when Brijesh Patel joined him and a scintillating stand of 139 runs ensued for the fourth wicket. Patel slammed sixteen boundaries during his innings of 83 and India's first innings, anchored by Sunil, was assured of a decent total.

The innings of 108 by Sunil was his tenth Test century, arriving in his thirty-second Test and sixty-first innings for India. An average of a century once every six innings, or once in three Tests, was a good striking rate by any standards but the significance of the figures lay in the future because Sunil was to double that standard in the next four years. While it had taken Sunil thirty-two appearances to reach double figures for centuries scored he would advance the total to twenty in little more than half that time. With the dawning of 1977, Sunil was entering the most productive phase of his career. The time had arrived when he was, without question, the master opening batsman. The first indication had been advertised with the 1,000 runs in 1976. Two months later the tenth Test century materialised and by the time that figure was doubled, in 1979, many a famous name from years gone by would be left floundering in his wake as one record after another tumbled to him.

As for the final Test, England made sound progress and

119

fell short of India's total by a marginal 21 runs on the first innings. When dismissing India comparatively cheaply for 192 at the second attempt a victory opportunity presented itself to the tourists but with the wicket taking spin the task became too severe for the England batsmen. Sunil had scored 42 to add to his century and continue in consistent vein. Unfortunately, it was with the ball, not the bat, that his name was to become the centre of attention for a heated argument broke out when he opened the bowling in the England second innings. The controversy raged because the England openers, particularly Amiss, alleged that Sunil was deliberately following through on to the pitch. The verbal exchanges became quite vociferous and the intentions of Amiss and Brearley were obvious. Sunil was allegedly attempting to create a 'spot' on the wicket for the slow bowlers to aim at. Eventually, the remonstrations between batsmen and bowler became so intense that the umpires had to intervene. Some time later Sunil put the matter into its correct perspective.

'Dennis Amiss is one of the nicest cricketers I've met but by the end of the series he was perhaps feeling the tensions and pressures of playing in India,' Sunil explained. 'It was understandable for him to blow his top but I think he lost it without reason. The only ball I followed through on the wicket was the one I bowled from near the stumps for which I was slightly warned, but it certainly wasn't deliberate. One can hardly create a spot in one or two overs.'

In fact, Sunil bowled only *one* over at the start of the England second innings but, in any event, the arguments made no difference to the result. Play ended in the fifth day with England hanging on grimly for a draw at 152 for 7 wickets, to take the series three–one, and a series which had begun catastrophically for India ended in a much better light. After the crushing defeats of the first three Tests the final outcome was far more satisfactory than anticipated. India had fought back with admirable gusto and the future, if not rosy, was better than the pundits had been declaring after the Third test.

With the Indian domestic season still in full flow there was little time for Sunil to reflect on his endeavours against England. Satisfaction of varying degrees could be gained from performances which had been a curious mixture of good, bad and indifferent. In the First Test Sunil's form had been reasonably good, followed by an uncharacteristic slump in the Second and Third. The Fourth Test brought a slight upsurge in fortunes and in the final match the cycle was complete with a polished century that signified his highest score to date against England. That innings was significant; in general Sunil's achievements were muted facing England. Compared to his record for India against other countries, it appeared that he could not 'put it all together' when confronted by English bowlers, although his aggregate of 394 runs was the highest he had yet achieved in any of four series against England.

Taken overall the figures were a trifle disappointing for a batsman of Sunil's calibre. From a total of sixteen appearances Sunil had scored 979 runs off the England attack at an average of 31·58 per innings, against a career Test average of 49·52. The situation was paradoxical. Whilst Sunil's Test reputation was steadily increasing, he seemed vulnerable against English bowling. It was true that he had picked off two centuries from the English attack but the same could be said about New Zealand and he had encountered the latter country only six times, not sixteen as against England. On the surface, the claim seemed valid. But Sunil had still to meet Australia and Pakistan at Test level and until then comparisons of relative performances were meaningless. The true picture would emerge when all the Test countries had been met.

On a more positive note, another aspect of Sunil's play was assuming far greater prominence, brought to the fore with particular clarity as the England series drew to a close. This was his fielding ability, a much improved facet of his game. He held seven catches in the five Tests, easily the best figure Sunil had achieved since his debut. In total, he had 27 Test catches to his credit, nearly all close to the wicket. Ironically, against England Sunil was at his best as a fielder and had twice held three catches in a single innings and this asset was gaining in importance to the present Indian team. With the decline of Eknath Solkar, a phenomenal short-leg fielder, India needed specialist close-catchers to replace him. Solkar's record in Test cricket was tremendous: he snapped up 53 catches in only 27 appearances and as he faded from the limelight India were fortunate to have dependable fielders like Sunil, Vishwanath and Yajuvindra Singh to replace him. Like Solkar, Sunil too would reach the worthy milestone of 50 Test catches, a feat achieved by comparatively few out-fielders from any country.

By an odd coincidence, the year of the fiftieth catch would be 1979, at approximately the same time as Sunil ended his lack of success against England. There was a time lapse of a few months and the catch would mark only one of many records that Sunil would bypass in 1979. They would arrive principally via a barrage of boundaries, the twentieth Test century, a third double century, a record-breaking opening partnership. The twentieth century was the key to Sunil's achievement. At the end of the 1976–7 England series, he had ten Test hundreds to his credit. Therefore, in little more than two years, the number would be doubled. The year of 1976 may have been extremely good for Sunil but he was only just beginning to set the cricket world alight. Records, records and more records, that was what lay ahead for Sunil.

The route to the goal began with a return trip to Australia. That was during the 1977–8 season and would be the starting point of another supercharged bout of run-scoring. Sunil had been Down Under once before, with a World XI, but this tour was a much more intense affair. There was a full-blooded, five-match Test series to play. Sunil was more than equal to the task. He was not there very long before he began gathering runs in his now accepted manner.

Prior to the Australian tour there was a season at home to finish (1976–7) and the following one to begin. He scored a century in each period for both Bombay and West Zone. Tamil Nadu were the first to suffer, to the tune of 120 runs in the Ranji semi-final of 1976–7 which Bombay predictably won easily against New Delhi. Following that run-spree, Sunil took 169 off the South Zone attack in the Duleep Trophy at the start of the next season. The latter century was made shortly before leaving for Australia. It augured well for the tour; Sunil was batting soundly and had every intention of adding several more centuries to the thirty-three already to his credit in his first-class career to date. Not surprisingly, he accomplished just that.

Averages for 1976–7 series v England, 5 Tests, played 5

Tests	Inns	NO	Runs	HS	Average	Bowling: 5–3–2–0
5	10	0	394	108	39·40	Fielding: 7 ct

Results: India 1, England 3, 1 Test drawn

Accumulative record

Tests	Inns	NO	Runs	HS	Average	Bowling: 26–8–65–0
32	62	5	2,776	220	48·70	Fielding: 27 ct

11   A Dramatic Series

Australia beckoned a second time for Sunil in 1977. On his
first visit, with the World team, he had not made a first-class
century, although he batted with sound skill and competence.
Now, seven years later and with ten Test hundreds to his
name, Sunil put the record straight in dashing style.

He scored a century in each of the First, Second and Third
Tests. They were an unusual trio, not only because they came
in three successive games but of the two other rather odd
circumstances that went with them. Firstly, each hundred was
scored in the second innings of the respective match in question and secondly, Sunil made no positive show in any of the
corresponding first innings involved. For the three matches
his scores read as follows: 3, 113, 4, 127, 0, 118. Counting
his 108 against England in Bombay in February 1978, Sunil
had registered four centuries in four consecutive Tests and
that was no mean feat by any standards, even when the
accompanying low scores in the same period are taken into
consideration.

The Australian series commenced at Brisbane, the usual
opening venue, where the first of several very closely fought

22 West Indies *v* India: a mistimed stroke ends Gavaskar's innings in the Prudential Cup match at Edgbaston. Andy Roberts was the bowler and the catch was taken by Michael Holding.

23 This was Ian Botham's 100th Test wicket. Mike Brearley has taken the catch which dismissed Sunil Gavaskar for 59 in India's second innings at Lord's, 1979.

games took place. Taking strike first, the Aussies fell dramatically to the spin of Bedi to be all out for 166 runs, in less than a day. The Indians could not have wished for a better start but they did not take the opportunity. Sunil made no more than three before he received a fiercely lifting ball from Australian newcomer Clark and Cosier accepted the chance in the slips. The second wicket fell with 15 on the board on the second day and, although Vengsarkar and Vishwanath tried to retrieve the situation, the Indians crumbled when they were parted. This pair added 75 runs, taking the total to 90 for 3 but from that point the remaining batsmen could take the score only to 153 all out.

A golden opportunity had been wasted. After dismissing the opposition so cheaply the Indian batsmen had failed to take the slightest of leads, which should have been a formality under the circumstances. The match was in fact still very evenly balanced with the negligible difference of thirteen runs separating the teams but, notwithstanding this, by the end of the game the Indian batting failure in the first innings was to prove decisively costly.

When Australia took strike a second time, wickets continued to fall at a rate rarely associated with Test Matches. Three men were rapidly sent back to the pavilion with only 2 runs to share between them and a scant 7 on the scoreboard. This brought the veteran Bobby Simpson to the crease (recalled to lead the side because of the Packer crisis) and with Ogilvie and Toohey as ample back-up support he led his team to comparative safety. Simpson made 89 but when Australia's ninth wicket fell at 277 there was still a danger of defeat. The lead was not particularly huge: a total of less than 300 was easily attainable, yet India once again insisted on throwing away the initiative.

A last-wicket partnership of 50 runs was allowed to be hit by Thomson and Hurst which, in conjunction with the first batting collapse, effectively lost India the match. A winning total of 341 runs was a significant mountain to climb in the fourth innings of any Test and it was not surprising that India failed to reach it. Failed, however, would be an unfair description of their efforts. The remarkable Indian quality for fighting back against all the odds was brought to the fore and, characteristically, Sunil led the way.

In a patient, dogged battle of an innings Sunil kept the Australian attack at bay while 243 runs were added to India's score. His own contribution amounted to 113, his maiden century in Australia, and he watched others come and go during the lengthy exercise. Of his varied partners, Mohinder Amanath and Vishwanath were the most reliable: 81 runs for the second wicket were added with the former while 59 accrued from the family liaison with the latter. On Sunil's departure at the fall of the sixth wicket another 98 runs were needed but for all his determined striving it appeared that the end was imminent.

The eighth wicket fell at 275 but then Kirmani and Bedi stubbornly added 43 to the total and India were within 23 runs of an exciting victory. It was a brave effort but, after Kirmani mishooked a bumper, Australia had little difficulty in dismissing Chandrasekhar and taking the match by 16 runs. The final margin was desperately close, with either side in with the opportunity to claim the spoils. Victory could, perhaps should, have been achieved, but defeat was the penalty for too many missed opportunities at earlier stages of the match.

The Second Test at Perth also produced a very close finish with Australia again clinching the verdict, on this occasion by 2 wickets, to go two–nil up in the series. Whereas at Brisbane both sides had batted badly in the early flourishes the Perth game was very different. In a particularly high-scoring game a pulsating cricket match was concluded with a winning hit which came with just twenty-two deliveries remaining. All the more remarkable was that a decisive finish was possible at all for 1,468 runs in all were scored over the full five days of play. Seldom do such high-scoring matches

128

produce anything better than dull, lifeless draws and the result was a credit to both teams, giving Test cricket its best advertisement possible.

The high scoring by both teams can be judged from India's second innings total of 330 for 9 wickets declared. It was the lowest made by either side in the whole match! Sunil's major contribution came in this innings, when he made 127. Much of the innings was shared with Mohinder Amanath, who also reached three figures and participated in a very large second-wicket partnership which realised 193 runs. The full scorecard of this remarkable match is shown on pages 130 and 131.

Sunil's second century of the series unfortunately coincided with India's second defeat. To go to Melbourne for the Third Test two games down was a daunting prospect for the Indians but they were nothing if not resilient. They had never won a Test in Australia, were now on the verge of losing the series in three straight games yet proceeded to trounce the Aussies by some 222 runs. What an unpredictable team they are!

Sunil attained his novelty 'hat-trick' at Melbourne by making 118 in the second innings following a nought at the first attempt. Bedi had taken first choice of the wicket only to watch in despair as not only Sunil but Chetan Chauhan went without a run on the board. Mohinder Amanath and Vishwanath rescued their team with a timely century partnership, the basis of India's eventual total of 256 all out. In view of the result it seems surprising that Australia were beaten so convincingly and by so great a margin. The Indian first-innings total was not overwhelming by any standards and the Australians should have been quite confident at that stage of the game.

The home batting did not, in the event, reflect much confidence at all. Chandrasekhar bowled with great aplomb, taking 6 for 52, and India gained a marginal 43-run lead. The opportunity to take a strong initiative was there again for India and on this occasion it was not cast aside. With Sunil as the foundation, a match-winning score was built in the

Australia v India

Second Test, 16, 17, 18, 20 & 21 December 1977 at Perth,

India

	1st Innings		2nd Innings	
S. M. Gavaskar	ct Rixon b Clark	4	b Clark	127
C. P. S. Chauhan	ct Gannon b Simpson	88	ct Ogilvie b Thomson	32
M. Amanath	ct Gannon b Thomson	90	ct Rixon b Simpson	100
G. R. Vishwanath	b Thomson	38	ct Rixon b Clark	1
D. B. Vengsarkar	ct Rixon b Clark	49	ct Hughes b Gannon	9
B. P. Patel	ct Rixon b Thomson	23	b Gannon	27
S. M. H. Kirmani	ct Rixon b Thomson	38	lbw b Gannon	2
S. Venkataraghavan	ct Simpson b Gannon	37	ct Hughes b Gannon	14
S. Madan Lal	b Gannon	43	b Thomson	3
B. S. Bedi	b Gannon	3	not out	0
B. S. Chandrasekhar	not out	0	not out	0
Extras	b1 nb8	9	b1 lb4 nb10	15
	Total	402	Total (for 9 wkts dec)	330

Fall of Wickets

	1	2	3	4	5	6	7	8	9
	14	163	224	229	235	311	319	383	391
	47	240	244	283	287	289	327	328	330

Bowling

Bowling	O	M	R	W	O	M	R	W
Thomson	24	1	101	4	21·5	3	65	2
Clark	17	0	95	2	18	1	83	2
Gannon	16·6	1	84	3	18	2	77	4
Mann	11	0	63	0	8	0	49	0
Simpson	11	0	50	1	8	2	41	1

Australia

Batsman	1st Innings	Runs	2nd Innings	Runs
J. Dyson	ct Patel b Bedi	53	ct Vengsarkar b Bedi	4
C. S. Serjeant	ct Kirmani b Madan Lal	13	ct Kirmani b Madan Lal	12
A. D. Ogilvie	b Bedi	27	b Bedi	47
P. M. Toohey	st Kirmani b Bedi	0	ct Amanath b Bedi	83
R. B. Simpson	ct Vengsarkar b Venkataraghavan	176	run out	39
S. J. Rixon	ct Kirmani b Amanath	50	lbw b Bedi	23
K. J. Hughes	ct Patel b Bedi	28	lbw b Madan Lal	0
A. L. Mann	ct Vengsarkar b Bedi	7	ct Kirmani b Bedi	105
W. M. Clark	ct Patel b Chandrasekhar	15	not out	5
J. R. Thomson	ct Amanath b Venkataraghavan	0	not out	6
J. B. Gannon	not out	0		
Extras	lb25	25	b8 lb10	18
Total		394	(for 8 wkts)	342

Fall of Wickets

	1	2	3	4	5	6	7	8	9
1st	19	61	65	149	250	321	341	388	388
2nd	13	33	172	195	295	296	330	330	

Bowling

Bowler	O	M	R	W	O	M	R	W
Madan Lal	15	1	54	1	11	0	44	2
Amanath	16	2	57	1	3	0	22	0
Chandrasekhar	33·6	2	114	1	15	0	67	0
Bedi	31	6	89	5	30·2	6	105	5
Venkataraghavan	23	4	55	2	28	9	86	0

Result: Australia won by 2 wickets

second innings. Useful contributions were made by several other batsmen and 343 all out set Australia a stiff target of 387 runs to win. Sunil's sixteenth century in Test cricket was a timely springboard towards success for his side. It was achieved in his thirty-fifth Test appearance and sixty-eighth innings, figures which justified his world status. Sunil, statistically, was averaging a century at a rate very nearly of one every second Test in which he played. But another way, on an innings-by-innings basis, the average was 4·25, or a hundred on every fourth or fifth occasion he walked to the crease.

With the batting accomplished, Chandrasekhar took to the stage. He gave an exact repeat performance of his earlier effort, claiming the same 6 for 52 and Australia were hustled out for 164 runs. Against a Chandrasekhar in full flight, the home side did not at any time appear to have the remotest chance of making the required runs. The final margin of defeat was a crushing blow to a team who had not lost any of the previous Tests played against India in Australia and after waiting thirty years for the first taste of success, the flavour was very sweet indeed for the Indians.

By virtue of the victory India pulled away from the brink of disaster in the series. In the Fourth Test, at Sydney, the team went one better. Australia were comprehensively thrashed by an innings and suddenly the series was all-square. It was a tremendous fight-back by the tourists but to a certain extent at Sydney the Indians were aided by some appallingly weak-willed Australian batting in their first innings. Their total of 131 all out handed the game to India on the first day, for by close of play Sunil and Chetan Chauhan had scored 80 without being parted and India were in command.

On the second day Sunil was caught behind the wicket one short of his half-century but little 'Vishy' soon took over the mantle of leading batsman. He top-scored with 79, while Ghavri (64), Vengsarkar (48) and Kirmani (42) all made runs to enable Bedi to declare at 396 for 8 wickets. The one innings was sufficient: Australia were a well-beaten side. They per-

132

formed with far more distinction in the second innings, particularly Toohey who hit 85, but defeat was inexorable. Australia required 265 runs to save the humiliation of an innings defeat; they managed 263 and, albeit by a mere two runs, ignominy was duly inflicted on the home side by India, to set the stage for an all-or-nothing fight in the last Test at Adelaide.

Another feast of run-scoring from both teams was the recipe for the last Test of an evenly fought exciting series. Australia began with a mammoth 505-run total and India concluded the game by making 445 all out, a record losing total in the second innings of a Test match. In all, 1,475 runs were scored in the match with Australia emerging as the victors by 47 runs. As in both of the previous home victories, the difference between the teams at the end of the games was desperately close. How ironic it was that in both of India's successes they had completely overwhelmed Australia. Defeat could so easily have been victory in any of the three lost Tests, in addition to the series as a whole.

Despite the flurry of runs Sunil had a quiet game in the final Test. During Australia's first innings he held two catches. Other than that he did little of note in the rest of the game. India made 269 all out in reply to the Aussie's 505, of which Sunil scored 7 and in the second innings 29. India were then chasing a total of 493 runs to win, after dismissing Australia for 256 and Sunil's early dismissal was a severe blow to the tourists. Victory was not at all likely, and a draw only a remote possibility. There were fourteen hours of play remaining when India began batting a second time. Without Sunil, India's hopes seemed gone.

Everybody was to be proved wrong. On the final day each of the batsmen played a part, including those who would not normally be recognised as such. Nobody reached three figures in the score of 445 but everybody contributed significantly and, while the end-result was never really in doubt, India put up a sterling performance to come to within 50 runs of a huge

133

target. Whatever justifiable criticism could often be cast upon the Indian batsmen at times there was no question about their ability to fight back. Time and again they had done it, almost as if it was an Indian hallmark, and they would go on doing the same in the future: the Oval 1979 would be the perfect example. But unfortunately the same players seemed unable to hold their game together over a whole match. Once again Sunil's own words were proving to be so very true. 'They never seem to play to their full potential.' Full was the key word; if India performed to that potential they would be a force to be reckoned with against any Test side.

After a magnificent start to the tour Sunil ended his sojourn in Australia quietly. The Indian team had performed unexpectedly well after the early reverses, while Sunil personally had touched peak form on numerous occasions. He was rapidly becoming a master opening batsman, recognised as such by the Test bowlers of the world, if not yet by the critics. Next on the horizon was an intriguing series later in the year. October 1978 would mark the resumption of sporting contact with near-neighbours Pakistan.

The Pakistan series was to be all-important to Sunil, the undoubted launching-pad to story-book, fairy-tale feats. He was on the verge of cricketing greatness, as he had been for several years but with the Pakistan series came the moment of realisation. Perhaps the Pakistan series would not prove it conclusively at one step but a few weeks after came confirmation, if any was still needed. Nevertheless, the Indo-Pak Series of 1978 would certainly open the floodgates for Sunil, floodgates that would bring a cascade of runs from his bat in a profusion not seen since the days of Bradman. Yet perhaps even the mighty Don did not match the run-getting achievements of Sunil in the hectic, latter months of 1978 and early part of 1979. Undeniably Sunil reached heights unknown previously in Test cricket. Comparisons are worth little. Sunil can stand by his own standards.

Averages for 1977–8 series v Australia, 5 Tests, played 5

Tests	Inns	NO	Runs	HS	Average	
5	9	0	450	127	50·00	Bowling: 2–0–7–0
						Fielding: 8 ct

Results: Australia 3, India 2

Accumulative record

Tests	Inns	NO	Runs	HS	Average	
37	71	5	3,226	220	48·87	Bowling: 28–8–72–0
						Fielding: 35 ct

12   The Floodgates Open

When, in February 1978, Sunil returned from Australia he was within touching distance of nearly all the major Indian batting records. A number had already been passed, the most important being his personal total of thirteen Test centuries. This was one more than the previous record, formerly held by P. R. Umrigar. At the age of twenty-eight Sunil had every opportunity to make the record his own for a good many years to come. If he maintained a striking rate remotely near the present rate an Indian record would be established that very few batsmen would be able to approach in the future. Also, once the total reached fifteen or sixteen Sunil would be amongst a rather select company in the world order.

The next target was the record Indian Test aggregate, also held by Umrigar, who had accumulated 3,631 during his career. After Australia Sunil lay second. The tour had seen him steadily pass three former Indian players of high repute until a modest 405 runs was all that separated Sunil from Umrigar. As century followed century in Australia the aggregates of M. A. K. Pataudi, C. G. Borde and Vijay Manjrekar had fallen to Sunil. With age and time both on his side the final extent of his Test Match harvest of runs was sufficient to delight a cricket statistician.

An excuse often offered in explanation for modern players being able to break records previously thought unattainable is that more Test cricket is now played. This is true but the sheer volume of cricket, especially noticeable since the beginning of the 1970s, is not the sole reason for a player such as Sunil becoming a leading runmaker. While the extra Tests assist a batsman to compile large aggregates there is one prime fact to take into account when judging the worth of a particular performance: the actual number of Tests played by an individual in achieving a record of any description. Sunil provided the perfect illustration, when he passed Umrigar's mark of twelve Test centuries.

Umrigar made fifty-nine Test appearances for India. No matter how quickly one series follows another, Sunil had claimed the Indian Test-century record for himself after thirty-five appearances and, when the aggregate record was passed, Sunil was playing in his fortieth game for India. Moreover, in achieving both records, Sunil batted on considerably fewer occasions than Umrigar, the difference in the second instance being seventy-seven innings compared to Umrigar's ninety-four. Not surprisingly, Sunil's average was approximately ten runs higher per innings than Umrigar's at the end of his career 42·22, while Sunil's was 51·73 and climbing steadily.

There were two series planned for the 1978–9 Indian season, one abroad and one a much longer affair. Together the series would catapult Sunil into the world headlines. From being a great Indian player with a worldwide reputation, he would move to a level attained by no other batsman. In an eight-year Test career of great achievement, nothing that had gone before could compare with what Sunil was to do in the months ahead.

The assault on cricket history began on 16 October at Faisalabad in Pakistan. Sunil was about to embark on a run-spree of such colossal proportions, on so brief a time-scale, that it is one of the very few sporting records that may well stand for all time; indeed it is difficult to imagine *any* batsman making an impression. From 16 October to the culmination 78 days later was the timespan.

The venue was historic. The simple fact that India was playing a Test Match at Faisalabad alone made the game very different from any other: the First Test of the three-match series was the first such encounter between the two countries for eighteen years. Politics had caused the initial rift in 1960 and since then the teams had gone their separate ways. A resumption of cricketing contact could only be of benefit to the game in general but from the often stormy events on the field throughout the series it was obvious that very little love existed between the two sides.

The best that could be said was that India and Pakistan were playing together again and, given the current political circumstances, it was perhaps unavoidable that the series would be tense. Previous encounters had always produced fiercely patriotic competition and there was little evidence to show a wish for a trouble-free series. Nevertheless, harsh words were spoken at times and some of the incidents which occurred were far from generally accepted Test-cricket practice. Especially in the light of his previous brushes with authority and the odd appearance before committees of inquiry, it was almost inevitable that Sunil would be at the forefront of the on-the-field hostilities.

The 1979 series was only the fourth between India and Pakistan, since the latter attained Test status in 1952. Pakistan's first-ever Test series was against India in that year, when India triumphed by two games to one in a five-match rubber. The Fourth and Fifth Tests were drawn and from that moment stalemate set in between the two teams. A second series was played in 1954, followed by another in 1960, each over five Tests, but not one definite result was forthcoming in any of the games. Thus, a depressing sequence of twelve con-secutive drawn matches had been played out. The sole point this emphasised was the fervent nationalistic element always

138

present whenever the teams met. Competition ceased after 1960. In many ways cricket was well served by this political decision because there was little point in playing Test matches that were certain draws long before a ball was bowled. Why this state of affairs should exist is impossible for a foreigner to understand fully but neutrals really have no right to pass comment on the inter-country rivalry always apparent between India and Pakistan.

The subject is so complex only the people directly involved can reasonably be expected to understand the intricacies of it all. It is not simply a matter of cricket, or politics, or religion or national pride but also the whole host of other imponderables which enter into the debate and take it far beyond simplistic, clear-cut thinking. Consequently, the final word is best left to a player, namely, Sunil, from within one of the rival camps.

'A cricket series between India and Pakistan is perhaps like the fight for the Ashes between England and Australia', Sunil explained. 'In the earlier series the attitudes of the captains and players was to first ensure that they never lost so there were more draws than necessary. At the same time, the Indian and Pakistan teams were well-matched, so it was difficult to arrive at decisions on the kind of true wickets they had then.' Significantly, Sunil added a final comment, 'However, there is no doubt that an Indo-Pakistan series has a special flavour of its own.'

The final comment was a reminder of the always-prevalent explosive atmosphere when the two teams met but before the series proper began, Sunil flexed his muscles against less formidable opposition. With the unlikely sounding name of 'Pakistan Banks XI' observers could be forgiven for thinking such a team was not first-class, but with several players of international repute in the line-up the fixture did hold senior status. Sunil took the opportunity for some gentle batting practice, hitting 165 not out and registering the thirty-seventh century of his career. Next came the start of the series at

Faisalabad. It would be none-too-pleasant at times, particularly for Sunil, but when the arguments and recriminations had faded away the Pakistan–India series of 1978 would be remembered most of all for what he himself achieved and began to achieve during it.

Tension began to mount from the earliest moments of the First Test. Taking first use of the pitch, Pakistan did not declare until 503 runs were on the scoreboard for the loss of 8 wickets. A draw was in prospect immediately, although the Pakistan innings had passed without any major mishap. The scene changed dramatically when India began their reply, with Sunil and Chetan Chauhan opening the innings. A constant stream of bumpers were directed at the pair, the chief culprit being Pakistan's pace bowler Sarfraz Nawaz. After some time Sunil called for his captain to come on to the field. At the appearance of Bishen Bedi the watching pressmen leaped straightaway to the conclusion that Sunil was protesting about intimidatory bowling and flashed the news around the world. The tale was given added credence when Sarfraz was taken out of the attack when Bedi returned to the pavilion but the newshounds were badly off target with their choice of subject material. Bedi's discussion with Sunil decided a matter no more serious than what the correct time was at that particular moment.

'I called Bishen on to the pitch because the watches of the umpires were not synchronised,' Sunil explained. 'In fact, there was a difference of twenty minutes between the watches of the umpires and as there was no clock on the ground I had to establish whose time we were going by.' As for the short-pitched bowling, the answer was simple: 'I don't think Chetan and I were bothered by bumpers because we thought it was a waste of a new ball.'

There ended problem number one. Whoever heard of a Test Match cricket ground without a clock! Negotiations saved the day and Sunil continued, scoring 89 before being dismissed and proving that the bumpers held no terrors for him. The following Indian batsmen also played adequately and, although a first-innings lead was not attainable, when Bedi declared at 462 for 9 wickets the game was doomed to be a draw. It was the thirteenth successive statemate in Indo-Pakistan meetings but the fun and games were far from finished in this game, whatever the result. The second major incident occurred when play was supposed to begin on the last morning: the weather was perfect, the players were ready but there was not an umpire in sight! Something very untoward must have happened to bring this about and, true to form, Sunil was at the heart of the matter.

It transpired that the umpires had decided to take impromptu strike action because of a remark Sunil had made the previous day. During the early part of the Pakistan second innings one of the officials, Shakoor Rana, had spoken to an Indian bowler for running on the wicket. At this, Sunil passed an obviously forceful comment which had the unfortunate outcome of making the umpire feel 'slighted'. It would be interesting to know the exact nature of Sunil's words, what form of Eastern invective could invoke such drastic action but, whatever the words were, it was enough to halt a Test Match!

Later, it was publicly announced that the wrangle had been resolved with a handshake. It must have been a very long one because play was more than fifteen minutes late in starting after the problem first arose! The humour of the situation did not appeal to Sunil's often mischievous sense of fun when the point was put to him.

'Well that particular umpire was so biased it was not funny', Sunil remarked, 'but then I was at fault because I should have kept my cool. Amazingly, this umpire did not make any protest that evening. Instead, he waited until the next morning and got the headlines he wanted. Funnily, when the watches incident occurred, he chided me for attracting public attention.'

There ended problem number two. That one was diplomatically shaken out of the way. The delay made no difference to the result. Pakistan declared at 264 for 4 wickets and India had no time left to make any sort of challenge for victory. Sunil and Chauhan casually batted out time, scoring 43 without being parted. For numerous reasons the match would not be amongst the fondest of Sunil's memories but he could still have the last laugh. In addition to scores of 89 and 8 not out, another startling event took place in the Pakistan second innings for which Sunil had waited since he played in his first Test Match, nearly eight years earlier. It was his first Test wicket. The prize was no less a batsman than Zaheer Abbas and, to add insult to injury, the gifted Pakistan batsman was on 96 at the time.

Lahore staged the Second Test where, finally, a decisive result was obtained but once again ill-temper marred proceedings. The destiny of the match was sealed by India's modest first-innings total of 199 all out, to which Pakistan replied with the huge score of 539 for 6 wickets declared. The most India could hope to gain from the match was a draw but, in the face of such a deficit, it was a doubtful proposition. Undaunted, and eager to make amends for a first-innings lapse which produced only 5 runs, Sunil took guard a second time, with Chauhan as his partner, determined to lift India from the seemingly hopeless position. When the pair had put together an opening partnership of 192·runs it appeared that India might indeed achieve a highly creditable draw but at that point two very contentious decisions were made by the umpires, which involved both openers, and controversy was in the headlines again.

Chauhan went first, followed a few moments later by Sunil, who was so incensed at being given out caught at point that he thrashed his bat into the ground at every step he took on the way back to the pavilion. Normally the most even-tempered of sportsmen, Sunil made clear his feelings in no uncertain manner. His score was on 97 but that was not the main reason for his displeasure. There could be every justification for feeling he had been cheated out of another Test century.

24, 25, 26 & 27 *(this page and overleaf)* The fourth Test at the Oval, 1979.
Sunil Gavaskar demonstrates a magnificent range of strokes.

However, as he never looks at the scoreboard when batting the claim could not be made that he was merely acting in a petulant manner. No, Sunil's show of outrage was caused by sheer annoyance.

'I was annoyed because we were making a terrific fight-back', said Sunil. 'First Chetan was the victim of a bad decision and then it was me.' He added, when asked about the missed century, 'I didn't know I was on 97 because I never look at the scoreboard. In fact, I thought I was out in the 80s.'

There ended problem number three, not at all happily resolved as were, to some degree, the earlier brushes with authority. Deprived of their openers, India continued to battle away. The final total of 465 all out was an excellent second-innings performance but it gave Pakistan a relatively simple task to gain victory. The target was 126 runs, reached with 8 wickets to spare and, for the first time since 1952, a Test Match between India and Pakistan had produced a result at a fourteenth attempt. Sadly, there had to be more than a little rancour involved in the process.

From Lahore the teams travelled to Karachi for the last of the three Tests. Another 8 wicket victory meant Pakistan won the series by two games to nil. For the Indians it was a disappointment but, when considering the part played by Sunil in the game, the result could be classed as being of secondary importance. His personal success more than compensated for the defeat, if only for the fact that Sunil had raised his name to be included with those truly exceptional in the long history of Test cricket. The means by which he accomplished this rapid promotion were a century in each innings of the Karachi Test. Sunil had scored two centuries in the same Test once before, against West Indies some seven years earlier, and in doing so joined approximately two dozen other players. Twenty-four, or thereabouts, is not a particularly high number of players, notwithstanding the worth of the achievement, when bearing in mind the hundreds of Test Matches that have been played since they first began in 1877 in Australia. Consequently, that particular list makes quite select reading.

Sunil had now performed the feat *twice*, thereby joining an even more select band of players who, with his own name added, numbered only five. This put Sunil in eminent company and, for the devotees of Bradman, who sometimes shrink away from the thought of the Indian master being bracketed with him, it is worth noting that even he, the all-time master, performed the feat only once, against India in 1948.

One record did escape Sunil at Karachi. His first innings score of 111 gave him the notable distinction of having hit a century against every Test-playing country, but he was not the first Indian batsman to complete the set. That honour had gone to his close friend and brother-in-law, Gundappa Vishwanath. It was certainly a novel way to keep the record in the family. The second hundred had another significance apart from being his second of the match. The 137 runs Sunil scored were more than sufficient to take his Test aggregate passed 'Polly' Umrigar's. It was his final innings of the series, hoisting the aggregate to an all-time Indian high of 3,673 runs. Sunil was ahead of Umrigar by 42 runs, but with his twenty-ninth birthday still eight months away it was well within the bounds of possibility that Sunil would more than double the previous record.

The twin hundreds against Pakistan placed Sunil on his own as an Indian batsman. Of the present-day players only comrade-in-arms Vishwanath was anywhere near his record, either in terms of runs scored or centuries made in Tests. Six months was all that separated the pair in age, Vishwanath being the elder and having six more Test appearances to his credit than Sunil. On his debut against Australia, in 1969, Vishwanath hammered 137 runs off an above-average attack and for Sunil to give him half-a-dozen Tests' start and still leave him trailing, was a noteworthy achievement in its own right. Vishwanath, too, was every inch a world-class player. The indebtedness of the Indian team of the 1970s to this pair is incalculable: without them the position would have been hopeless. Fortunately, they were there, as bowlers around the world discovered to their cost.

What next for Sunil? Now that he stood alone on the Indian scene, within weeks of the Pakistan Series finishing his name would be in world prominence. In his present form, not a single opening batsman in the world could be compared with Sunil. For nearly eight years he had promised to break and establish batting records. In 1978 it began to happen, and with a rapidity so astonishing it almost caught the rest of the cricket world completely unawares.

Averages for 1978 series against Pakistan, 3 Tests, played 3

Tests	Inns	NO	Runs	HS	Average	
3	6	1	447	137	89·40	Bowling: 9–1–33–1
						Fielding: 3 ct

Results: Pakistan 2, India 0, 1 Test drawn

Accumulative record

Tests	Inns	NO	Runs	HS	Average	
40	77	6	3,673	220	51·73	Bowling: 37–9–116–1
						Fielding: 38 ct

13　The Spate Continues

Once back in India from the mini-tour of Pakistan there were but few days for the Indian players to spend in relaxation. A six-Test series against West Indies was scheduled to start on 1 December 1978, little more than two weeks after the conclusion of the Pakistan series. Significant changes were announced in the short interim period to the first West Indian Test. They concerned both teams and on the Indian side Sunil was directly involved.

Bishen Bedi was relieved of the captaincy and to his great joy Sunil was appointed successor to the mercurial left-arm spin bowler, who still maintained his place in the team. Sunil was thrilled at the honour, although he was not to know that his reign would be brief. Similarly, his return to the players' ranks would be equally short, providing a prime example of the topsy-turvy, often bewildering spate of changes that continually occur in Indian cricket.

In numerous ways the elevation to the captaincy, followed by summary swift demotion, were of little consequence. Sunil was rapidly approaching a zenith in his career. The West Indies series started at Calcutta on the opening day of December as planned and by the second day of January of the New Year Sunil would stand alone in the record books. There were three very important reasons (and records) why such a high ranking was attained.

As for the Test series, it went to India by virtue of a solitary victory and with five games drawn the immediate picture is of a rather dull series. However, the actual match details take second place on this occasion. Only the batting exploits of Sunil need be studied.

Everything began to happen during the First Test at Bombay in a drawn game which saw less than three innings completed. Sunil was outstanding in India's first innings. The home side totalled 424 all out, of which Sunil's contribution was a glorious double-century. This 205 was the second Sunil had taken off West Indies and, following the Pakistan series, was his third successive Test century. Once more Sunil was joining select company who had performed a similar feat.

Many critics rated this innings as the best of his career to date as he played with an attacking verve that he showed too rarely throughout his career.

A similar pattern emerged in the second Indian innings, after West Indies had scored 493 all out. A fourth consecutive century appeared a formality until he was caught behind the wicket off the bowling of Clarke for 73. The match was doomed to be a draw but Sunil was batting with irrepressible pugnacity. In this frame of mind there was no other opening batsman (or batsman of any description) in the world who was performing at anywhere near his level of consistency. Paradoxically, to prove that even the best cricketers are not entirely infallible, Sunil demonstrated the truth of the matter most emphatically.

The Second Test was at Bangalore. Another drawn game became a formality and, in India's solitary innings of 371 all out, Sunil was promptly dismissed first ball! It is easy to fall from grace but with a similar swiftness Sunil bounced back in the very next Test.

The game was played at Calcutta and while another draw

was not the best of results Sunil's personal performance was stunning. At the end of the day West Indies literally clung on to the game and survived because their last pair were at the wicket when time was called. However close it was, the West Indies did survive but of more importance was the batting skill displayed by Sunil.

The extent of his two-innings effort is as follows:

1 Sunil made scores of 107 and 182 not out. This meant he was the *only* batsman in the history of Test cricket ever to score a century in both innings of the same Test on *three* separate occasions.
2 In the second innings Sunil shared an unbroken record partnership of 344 runs with D. B. Vengsarkar. This is an Indian Test record partnership for the second wicket against any country.
3 By scoring 182 not out in the second innings Sunil had, between 16 October 1978 and 2 January 1979, scored the incredible total of 1,014 runs. The time-scale for this fantastic achievement was just 78 days, which was very nearly half the previous record held by the legendary Wally Hammond who passed 1,000 runs in 124 days in the 1930s.

The run-spree encompasses eleven innings from which four centuries, one double century and three scores above fifty were registered (plus a first-ball 'duck'!). From the eleven innings Sunil produced an average of 101·40 for each occasion he walked to the crease. The Boycotts, Chappells and Greenidges of this world may be excellent players, but even they could not equal such a degree of consistency. The performance was out of this world. Even in these jet-age days of very frequent Test cricket it is highly unlikely that a player will surpass the record. It belongs to Sunil Gavaskar and unless a very special train of circumstances occurs it will remain with him for ever.

Another feat achieved by Sunil in the record-breaking two-century Calcutta Test was to equal another record held by England's Ken Barrington. As the match at Eden Gardens was at the end of the year, a count of Sunil's run-scoring for the whole of 1978 showed he had scored 1,044 in the twelve-month period from January to December. This was the second occasion on which he had passed 1,000 runs in a calendar year and only Barrington had done the same. Furthermore, in 1979 Sunil would repeat the past and become the *only* player to achieve the milestone *three* times. It is little wonder that, with records such as these, Sunil Gavaskar can be called incomparable. Much though many people may disagree the facts speak for themselves.

The Fourth Test was played at Madras. It was the deciding game of the series, with India clinching a nerve-tingling 3-wicket victory over the Caribbean tourists but Sunil had fluctuating personal fortunes. The series had begun with a double hundred and a fifty in the first match, followed by a first-ball nought. Then came the absolute summit with twin hundreds at Calcutta. Now, it was back to mediocrity. The word does not belong in any definitive description of Sunil, yet with scores of 4 and 1 respectively at Madras such would appear to be the case. There was certainly an air of 'all or nothing' about Sunil's record in this six-Test series against West Indies.

Whatever Sunil achieved in the Madras match, it counted but little as long as the final result was in India's favour and that is exactly what transpired. A narrow victory was as good a result as they wanted and with it went a one–nil lead in the series, which was not to be relinquished. New Delhi staged the Fifth Test and there Sunil proved yet again how strange the fortunes of world-class batsman can be. He proceeded to thrash the long-suffering West Indies bowlers for another century!

The significance of the 120 scored in India's capital city was that it was the *tenth* century Sunil had scored against West Indies. This was far in excess of the number of hundreds any

151

other batsman had scored against that country. Indeed, many a Test batsman would be pleased to finish his Test career with ten centuries to his credit, let alone ten against one country.

Of added importance to the innings of 120 was that it was Sunil's eighteenth three-figure innings in Test cricket. This was the number that Sir Leonard Hutton scored during his illustrious career but whereas he had played over seventy Test matches, Sunil had yet to play in his fiftieth. Now the only batsmen who had scored centuries in Test cricket in greater profusion than Sunil was Sir Donald Bradman. Sunil was scoring centuries at the rate of better than one every fifth time he batted in a Test Match. The pundits could say whatever they wished about the great players of yesteryear but when only one, and Bradman at that, could better this average Sunil Gavaskar had to be the greatest contemporary opening batsman in world cricket. He undoubtedly was.

He had only one more opportunity to make runs against West Indies. It came in the Sixth Test where, in a rain-ruined match, each team batted only once. Sunil made 40 before falling to a catch behind the wicket and there ended a momentous series. Quite apart from India's winning 1–0 the series had finally proved Sunil Gavaskar a batsman of the highest order.

The one cloud on the horizon was a man named Kerry Packer. As a result of mild flirtations with World Series cricket Sunil would soon be stripped of the captaincy of India. For wicketkeeper Syed Kirmani it would be worse. He would lose his place altogether, although the Indian selectors would soon realise the folly of their decision. Syed would make a swift return to the team when it was seen that no other wicketkeeper in the country (perhaps also, in the world at that time) could replace him.

With Sunil the situation was slightly different. Such was his standing both with the Indian public and on the world stage that it was impossible to drop him from the team altogether.

Consequently he was merely demoted from captain. That would be for the overseas tour of England in mid-1979.

In June the second World Cup tournament would take place, followed by a four-Test series against England. If Sunil still had anything to prove in his illustrious career it was in England. In every other country Sunil had performed superbly but in England he had been somewhat muted. Now was the chance to put the record straight. It would be done, in a most emphatic manner, but the story would be an exact replica of 1976–77, when he first scored 1,000 Test runs in a calendar year.

On the former occasion the opposition had also been England. Then Sunil had waited until the very last opportunity to bat before clinching his record. It would be similar in 1979 but, when the final innings came, it was worth all the nail-biting and lost cash that the author endured throughout the summer. Oh, yes, and the summer of 1979 also brought the author face to face with Sunil Gavaskar for the first time. And that alone made this book worthwhile.

Averages for 1978–9 series v West Indies, 6 Tests, played 6

Tests	Inns	NO	Runs	HS	Average	Bowling:
6	9	1	732	205	91·50	Fielding: 2 ct

Accumulative Record

Tests	Inns	NO	Runs	HS	Average	Bowling: 37–1–116–1
46	86	7	4,405	220	55·75	Fielding: 40 ct

14 Triumph in England

The reaction of the Indian Board of Control to Sunil's flirtation with the Kerry Packer organisation was swift and punitive. He was summarily dismissed from the captaincy for the planned tour of England in mid-1979, during which India would participate in the second World Cup competition and a four-Test series against the home country. The irony of the situation was that, within weeks of the tour commencing, the long-drawn-out saga between Packer and the International Cricket Conference was settled. It would have made no difference at all if Sunil had signed for Packer but as the Board of Control made a decision it was too late, at the present time at any rate, to make an alteration. Consequently, Srinivas Venkataraghavan led the team in England and Sunil was not even made vice-captain, for that appointment went to Vishwanath.

Whatever feelings there were in India about Packer there could be no question of Sunil not making the trip to England. He was the foundation on which the vast majority of Indian totals were built and the opposition to be met on the tour was an England side positively rampant. Brearley's men had pieced together a magnificent string of victories dating back to

1976–7, when the teams had last met. Exactly how good England were was extremely difficult to pinpoint accurately. Every team they had played and defeated since 1976–77 had, to varying degrees, been affected by the Packer storm. The same applied to England also, and as they could do no more than win whenever they took to the field the record appeared quite imposing at first sight because the victories had been achieved with embarrassing ease.

The party chosen to represent India in England showed several changes from the side which completed the series against West Indies six months earlier. Some very well-known names from previous visits to England were missing and with so many new names present it was clear that the basic side that had served India throughout most of the 1970s was beginning to disintegrate. The first indication came with the omission of E. A. S. Prasanna, an hitherto valued member of the world-renowned quartet of spin bowlers. Venkataraghavan, as captain, Chandrasekhar and Bedi remained but they too, like Prasanna, were approaching the veteran stage of their careers. Of the trio who went to England only Venkataraghavan would keep his place when India's next series began, against Australia, commencing in September 1979, and this abrupt break-up of the brilliant foursome signified the end of an era in Indian cricket.

Another name deleted, although only temporarily in his case, was wicketkeeper Syed Kirmani, after playing in twenty-nine consecutive Tests for India. Vying for his place were two young hopefuls, Bharat Reddy and Surinder Ghanna while another youngster who promised much was Kapil Dev. He had played a number of Tests against West Indies in the previous series, displaying great all-round potential, and there was every indication that he could become the fastest bowler India had produced for decades.

On the batting front, English critics thought there was a lack of substance. The reasoning was that too much responsibility rested on Sunil and Vishwanath. Chauhan, Vengsarkar,

155

Gaekwad and Mohinder Armanath all had reputations in India but it remained to be seen whether they could perform equally well under English conditions. Not for the first time in the course of the summer were the sceptics to be proved wrong and by September, when the tour ended, a goodly number were having to eat their words.

For Sunil personally, the tour presented a strange paradox. He began in June with his reputation as high as it had been at any time in his career yet he still had something to prove to the English public. The four-match series was the last hurdle Sunil had to climb to finally stamp his name on Test cricket. Although more muted than in the past, the criticism still lurked in the background that he had never performed as devastatingly against England, or in England, as he had against other cricketing countries. Everyone is entitled to their opinion but, when a player visits a country with more than 4,000 runs and nineteen centuries to his credit in less than fifty Tests, the arguments against his ability have little force. Fortunately, this was to be the tour when Sunil would lay to rest, once and for all, the absurd notion that he could not play a major innings in England. It was accomplished in a single knock that had respected commentators praising it as one of the finest innings in Test history and with those recommendations ringing in his ears Sunil set the seal on his Test career.

As the tour began to unfold the prospects were not good. Before the Tests was the second staging of the Prudential World Cup competition, held over two weeks in June. This was the reason for the Test series being shortened from the customary five to four matches. From India's point of view, it would have been more to their liking if the one-day tournament had not been held at all. An extra five-day Test would have been infinitely more agreeable than any of the World Cup games played at Birmingham, Leeds or Manchester. The performances were nondescript, lack-lustre and in one instance, woefully weak. For the hordes of armchair critics waiting on the sidelines, the three results were the perfect justification of all their prophecies concerning the Indian hopes for the Test Matches later in the summer. Playing in Group A with West Indies, New Zealand and Sri Lanka, India lost each 60-over game heavily and a more depressing start to the tour was impossible to envisage. Defeat in the first match by the trophy holders West Indies was not a surprise but to lose also to the Kiwis and then to Sri Lanka, a team which did not hold Test status, was total disaster.

The opening one-day fixture was played at Edgbaston, where West Indies skipper Clive Lloyd chose the customary limited-over method of attack and asked India to bat first on winning the toss. In reaching 190 all out India batted reasonably well but their opponents, specialists in this form of cricket, brushed aside the total with derisory ease, losing only 1 wicket in the process. There was much speculation as to how Sunil would fare in his first innings of the summer in England, for tales of his winter exploits had preceded him. The expectancy was not fulfilled. Receiving a short ball from Roberts, which Sunil thought were not allowed in the competition, he was committed to a forward stroke when the ball suddenly rose alarmingly. A top edge resulted and a simple catch was spooned to fine-leg. It was an inauspicious start but there was plenty of time in which to make amends.

Vishwanath saved the day for India. His 75 contributed the major portion to India's total and it was an innings full of majesty, power and perfect timed strokes. Gordon Greenidge hit a thrilling 106 not out for West Indies yet, magnificent as that innings was, a number of the watching commentators placed Vishwanath's effort as the better of the two. It is always difficult to judge the 'man of the match'; people will always disagree with the final choice and in this match the selection of Greenidge was probably correct. His stroke-play was no less exhilarating than Vishwanath's and West Indies did win.

More important than personal awards was the next game against New Zealand which India had to win in order to stay in the competition. It was an exact repeat of the situation in the inaugural tournament four years earlier. Unfortunately, the result and the tale of woe in 1979 were a carbon copy of the 1975 exercise; the only difference being that the latter performance was, if anything, even worse.

With the Kiwis winning at Headingley to clinch their own semi-final place, India were left with a rather meaningless fixture against Sri Lanka to complete the trio of group matches in the competition. Meaningless? Perhaps, but by losing India reached the depths of despair. For a team holding only associate status in the ICC, the result provided valuable ammunition in their fight for elevation to full Test rank; it was, without question, a very fine performance by Sri Lanka but the result was exactly what the critics wanted: they flayed India's performance.

After much hot air being exhaled in debate the consensus of opinion was that India had as much chance of winning a Test in the coming series as there was of the Queen turning Roman Catholic. That may well have been correct but at that time of the year it was far too early to be making such sweeping predictions. Also, what the vast majority of people forgot was that England had no God-given right to win whenever they took to the field. Their success in the past counted for nothing when a new series began.

When India started playing the county sides in the period immediately preceding the First Test, form improved. The bowlers enjoyed some mild success and the batsmen began making runs. Suddenly, it became apparent that England might not have the easy ride widely forecast. Whether intentional or not, what transpired was astonishing. It all began a week before the First Test was due to begin when a concerted (and at times, almost hysterical) campaign was launched by the media against one of the Indian players. Whatever can be said in defence of the all-out attack, it is significance that the barrage began just seven days before the First Test. Perhaps certain critics were beginning to have second thoughts about the series.

The furore centred around Karsan Ghavri, India's left-arm

medium-pace bowler. Both press and television began a fierce analysis of the legality of his bowling action. Ghavri had struck two England batsmen (Brearley and Larkins) during India's game with MCC at Lord's, plus another player in a county match. Not insignificantly, Ghavri had also taken an above average number of wickets at the same time. When this coincided with Brearley's split nose and Larkin's broken finger, Ghavri was instantly labelled a thrower. In a Test career dating back to 1974 Ghavri's bowling action had never once been under close scrunity from umpires and he had toured Australia, New Zealand and England (in 1975) in the intervening period. Why the doubts should be raised in 1979 is difficult to understand but the motives behind the attack must be dubious. When all is said and done, if England were going to ride roughshod over the Indians in the Test Series it would not matter if they had half-a-dozen throwers in their team.

The worst part of the outburst came from an unnamed English player who was quoted in the press as stating unequivocally that Ghavri's action was illegal. In that statement MCC's golden rule of silence from all players under contract was broken. It was not surprising that the player's name was not revealed but if he was so certain of what he was saying why did he not have the courage of his convictions and allow his name to be printed also? One reason stands out above the others for hiding behind the cloak of anonymity: the £1,250 appearance fee that would surely have been forfeited if he had been dropped from the side for the First Test. MCC could have adopted no other course in dealing with a player who had made such public statements and it would have been entirely justified.

Quite apart from the monetary aspect another fact was becoming increasingly obvious. Whatever the final results of the Tests would be, at the end of June India were showing much-improved form and the prospects for an England walkover were diminishing rapidly. England had experienced three years virtually devoid of defeat, picking up tidy sums of prize money at the same time, but the plain fact was that they were about to meet a better Test side than in any of the previous three years. Consider the opposition of those years: in 1977 an Australian team disintegrating at the seams because of Packer; in 1978 a Pakistan XI that was barely first class followed by a New Zealand side later in the same summer that was little better; in 1978–9 another Australian team, definitely second-team standard compared to the great Aussie sides of the past. Perhaps the prospects were not too pleasing for some of the England players who would be taking part in the series, especially those who had reaped overrated reputations at the expense of second-rate Test opposition. To prove the point, after the First Test England never looked like beating India in the Second, Third and Fourth and in the last match they almost lost what would have been the most remarkable Test victory of all time.

To prove how pointless the week-long saga of complaint had been England trounced India in the First Test at Edgbaston. A victory margin of an innings and 83 runs showed that England had the necessary talent to win without resorting to underhand, shabby forms of gamesmanship to gain the result. India were handicapped in that Bedi withdrew on the morning of the match with a stiff neck and his replacement, Chandrasekhar, was only half-fit because of Achilles tendon trouble. He had been omitted from the original XI and as the match progressed it was clear that he was only a shadow of his former self. In addition to the absent Bedi and the struggling Chandrasekhar India were further seriously hampered when Mohinder Amanath strained his back on the first day. He could bowl only 13·2 overs and the Indian attack became so weakened that the England batsmen were able to enjoy a two-day run feast. India's cup of woe was full to overflowing as they toiled away in the field but there were a few bright spots on the bleak horizon.

Kapil Dev bowled quite magnificently on a wicket that gave him no assistance at all. A double century by the marvellously precocious Gower, 155 from Boycott and a lusty 83 from Gooch out of a total of 633 for 5 declared showed how benign the pitch was but Kapil Dev never gave up the fight. His reward for a marathon stint of forty-eight overs was all five England wickets to fall. The strapping 6-foot tall twenty-year-old was blatantly overbowled but Venkataraghavan had no alternative because of his acute shortage of bowlers.

Shortly after tea on the second day India began batting. The only aim was to save the follow-on, a target of 433 runs, and an innings defeat was already a distinct possibility. Chauhan fell with the score at 15 and although no more wickets were lost before close of play India's hopes for the third day were very slim. Sunil, in keeping with his form on the tour to date, was batting soundly. A week before the Test he had torn the Hampshire attack to shreds in an innings of two distinct phases. The first hundred runs took a shade more than four hours to compile followed by a whirlwind spell of batting which produced over 60 runs in 30 minutes. Similar aggression was not called for in the Test, a more tempered, solid defensive role was the order of the day and when play resumed on the third day that was precisely how Sunil batted.

Although Vengsarkar departed at 59, a promising third-wicket partnership developed between Sunil and Vishwanath. Sunil was visibly growing in confidence with every stroke but when 70 runs had been added disaster struck. Sunil played a ball gently to mid-wicket and immediately set off for a single but the fielder was the deadly accurate Randall. Too late Vishwanath sent Sunil back. He was hopelessly stranded and a sweet cameo of an innings was needlessly ended at 61, with a century there for the taking. Nobody wanted a hundred more than Sunil—'the elusive three figures' as he would wistfully refer to it by the end of the tour, and the trek towards the goal had some of the drama and pathos of a Shakespearian tragedy. There was humour too, as the author discovered as Test followed Test.

Overnight Sunil had 44 runs to his name. The wicket was

behaving perfectly and during a conversation at the Indian team's hotel on the evening of the second day's play the author foolishly remarked, 'You can go out there tomorrow and get a hundred.'

Sunil, in non-committal style, replied, 'Oh, I don't know, perhaps. We'll see tomorrow.'

He was not denying that the possibility was there to score a hundred, merely being practical and cautious. Not so the author. Casting caution to the winds, he had taken a generous shade of odds, 5-1 no less, that the deed was as good as done. With Randall's arrow-like return a blue note was credited to the profits of a well-known firm of bookmakers, but at least Sunil had nine more innings in the series in which to make amends.

With Sunil gone, Vishwanath continued to bat immaculately with some rather shaky support coming from Gaekwad. Then came the collapse. At 205 for 3 Vishwanath succumbed to the flight of Edmonds for 78 and for the addition of just 24 more runs another 3 wickets fell. The one spark of resistance was from Reddy, playing a splendidly dour innings in his first Test, and from Venkataraghavan who slammed two gigantic sixes in a last defiant flourish. It was not enough, Shortly after 6 pm on the third day India were bowled out for 207 runs, leaving Sunil and Chetan Chauhan an uncomfortable fifteen minutes to bat out before close as Brearley enforced the follow-on.

Not only did the pair remain together until close of play on day three but for long enough on the fourth day to suggest that India could score sufficient runs in the second innings to make England bat again. No wicket fell until after lunch, by which time 124 runs had been added for the first wicket. Once again Sunil passed the half-century with ease but at 68 received an unplayable delivery from Hendrick that took the outside edge and Gooch snapped up the chance. Another delightful innings was terminated, just as a lengthy stay at the crease seemed inevitable. Unfortunately for India, Sunil's dismissal signified the beginning of the end.

Vishwanath again batted admirably to record his second fifty of the match (both he and Sunil totalled exactly the same total, 129 runs, from the two innings) but once he was caught behind off Botham, making the score 227 for 5 wickets the game was virtually finished. Wickets tumbled alarmingly and on the stroke of six o'clock, almost one complete day's play exactly since the second innings began, India were all out for 253 runs, some 83 short of the required target. It was a crushing defeat, some of the batsman showing a distinct lack of application and, predictably, the critics dismissed the Indians as a team without a chance in any of the remaining Tests. On the Edgbaston evidence that was probably true but Sunil and Vishwanath alone had shown what they might achieve if either played a long innings. It would require only one or two of the other batsman to provide adequate support and the England bowlers would not find it quite as easy in the later Tests. In fact, that is precisely what did occur, but the pundits were too shortsighted or too partisan to see the possibility of its actually happening. There was to be one more easy phase, the first innings of the Second Test; for the rest of the series England would be the team to struggle.

In the county game before the Second Test, against Gloucestershire, Sunil reached another memorable milestone in his career. Playing at Bristol, he scored 116 in the first innings but it was not just one more century to add to the many that had gone before, this was the fiftieth of his first-class career. In comparison to notable Indian players of the past, it took Sunil past the 49 hundreds P. R. Umrigar had made in his career and equalled the number made by K. S. Duleepsinhji. Only two Indian batsmen had scored more hundreds: V. S. Hazare, with 57, and the legendary K. S. Ranjitsinhji with 72 centuries. Fifty may not appear to be a particularly high number but for an overseas player not playing in English county cricket the achievement was quite remarkable. In India, Sunil was lucky to take part in many more than a dozen first-class games a season. Even when a Test series was played there were not many more matches to add: the Ranji Trophy, the Duleep Trophy and the single Irani Cup fixture which comprised the Indian first-class season. Unlike an English counterpart, opportunities were strictly limited and to average five centuries a year in all first-class cricket was a high degree of consistency. Somewhat lacking in awareness, the English press failed to recognise the significance of the Bristol century and the record passed unnoticed. Perhaps if the name had been Boycott the situation would have been slightly different. Each hundred he scored dutifully received comment: 110, 111, or 112 etc. For Sunil, not a mention.

From Bristol to Lord's and a magnificent rearguard action by India when the cause appeared to be completely lost. Venkataraghavan won the toss for the only time in the series and thirty minutes after the tea interval must have been cursing his ill-luck. The first wicket fell with 12 on the board, the seventh at 96 and that was the end of the innings. The last 4 wickets failed to add a single run to complete a thoroughly miserable attempt to compile a reasonable first-innings total. Sunil top-scored with 42, Vishwanath made 21 and without them India would have been hard-pressed to reach 50. Yet the talent was there if only the Indian batsmen would exploit their resources. That would be proved conclusively long before the end of the series and it was not surprising that Sunil said his team-mates rarely played to their full potential when they could muster a paltry 33 runs amongst nine of them. Without Sunil and Vishwanath, India's hopes, on more occasions than the rest of the team would wish to remember, would have been non-existent.

The outcome of the first-innings shambles was that India had just two possibilities for salvation when Brearley declared the England innings closed at a quarter-past twelve on the fourth day. In either instance a draw would be the result if India succeeded. England held a lead of 323 runs, which ruled out any idea of an Indian victory. Therefore, India had to ensure that England were set a target beyond their reach in the time available *or* they had to bat out the better part of two whole days. Then England would not have any opportunity at all to bat a second time for victory. Typically, the critics dismissed both methods of escape as wishful thinking. They could see no further than an England win and, to underline the earlier assertions in this chapter about the biased, misguided chauvinism shown by the press, the following headline is the perfect example of their attitude:

EASY, EASY!

'As England's cricketers prepare for the formality of their second successive thrashing of India today . . . (*Daily Mirror*, 6 August 1979).

Sunil and Chetan Chauhan had other ideas. A first-wicket partnership of 79 runs gave India a sound start and in this respect India were infinitely better served than England, a fact conveniently overlooked when the series was analysed in retrospect. Chauhan went first, caught at short-leg by Randall but he clearly disagreed with the decision, thinking the ball had ricocheted off the pad. He had to go but Sunil continued to bat with authority. It was his fourth innings of the series and the fourth time he appeared to be in total command of the situation. Would this be the day of the century? Many thought so, including the author, once again foolish enough to bet on Sunil's chances at the less than generous odds of 9–4. The now customary half-century (his third in four innings in the series) was duly reached but at 59 Brearley brilliantly picked up, one-handed, a snick that travelled with the speed of a bullet from the edge of the bat. It was goodbye Sunil and goodbye cash. Of more importance was the score, 99 for 2 wickets.

Vishwanath was the incoming batsman and another wicket at that stage would place England well on top. In fact, although the time was only half-past three on the fourth day the game was practically over. Vengsarkar and Vishwanath were not parted until five minutes to five the next day. There were some interruptions for bad weather but the fighting performance by the pair was tremendous. Both hit centuries in a stand of 210 for the third wicket and finally, at the fourth attempt, the Indian batsman had found the measure of the England bowlers. Especially pleasing was the fact that someone other than Sunil or Vishwanath had made a sizeable score. Vengsarkar's 103 proved that India had other class batsman who could take the fight to England.

When play ended on the last day India had made 318 for 4 wickets to force a very honourable draw.

Indian confidence soared, while England's ego was slightly deflated, and the series no longer a mere formality. One innings had transformed Vengsarkar. In addition to the distinct promise shown by Yashpal Sharma, making his debut in the Second Test, India were putting a far stronger batting side into the field than many people had previously thought possible. Sunil and Vishwanath were still the linch-pins but they now had more than a useful back-up support, with several other players equally capable of taking sizeable scores off the England attack.

Sunil went into the Third Test at Headingley with a consistent record to his name in the previous games. Three half-centuries and one near miss gave him an average well above 50 but still the doubts lingered. Unfortunately, the Leed's Test would only add more fuel to the fire. In a match completely ruined by rain, much of the attention in the final stages was solely on Sunil as, once again, a century seemed certain. On the afternoon before the match another discussion took place between the author and Sunil regarding the likelihood. In common with what had gone before the conversation was to have the opposite effect to the one desired.

'How about it this time, Sunil?', I said, as we walked from the team's hotel on that damp, blustery Wednesday afternoon. 'You've looked like doing it every time you've batted up to now. Surely you can do it this time.'

166

'We'll see' was Sunil's reply. He gave a whimsical smile. 'It would be nice but this will have to change first', he added, looking up at the rain-laden skies.

It very nearly was 'nice' but Sunil's words were all too true. England batted first and it was not until 3 pm on the fourth day that the innings was completed. Rain, rain and more rain was the prelude, first movement and finale of the entire match. The century came not from Sunil but from England's Ian Botham, who, on the fourth morning despatched the Indian bowling to every part of Headingley in what was undoubtedly one of the most thrilling bouts of controlled hitting ever seen in a Test Match. In the pre-lunch period Botham advanced his score from 8 to 107 to fail by the narrowest of margins to become the first player since 1935 to hit a hundred before lunch in a Test. Anyone privileged to be present saw an innings of a kind unlikely to be repeated for many years as 5 sixes and 16 fours streamed from his bat. It was more than just wild hitting: the majesty that went with the power made the innings unique. Botham may be brash and possess an 'I am the greatest' attitude but when batting as he did at Headingley there are few who can argue against him.

Botham's 137 was the only worthwhile score in England's total of 270 all out. That was their lowest total of the series and it was a measure of India's luck during the summer that it had to occur in a Test drawn because of rain. However, as the weather had relented by the fourth day the opportunity was there for the Indian batsmen to utilise the remaining time for batting practice. Sunil began as if that was exactly what he had in mind. He was still at the crease when play began on the fifth morning, close to another fifty, and with the game predestined to conclude in stalemate, the longed-for century was, if anything, more likely than at any other time in the series.

In the meaningless draw, where both sides could manage only one innings apiece, a hundred for Sunil would be no more than a statistic in the record book. It would, nevertheless, help

167

fill the back pocket of the author, who had resolutely followed his all-season belief that a Gavaskar century was as good as fact and this time had invested a £10 note. When Sunil moved into the 70s, tension began to mount. This *had* to be the occasion; past form decreed it. Was it not true that in a forty-nine-Test career Sunil had only three times been dismissed between the scores of 75 and 100? Yes, it most certainly was, but of all the days Sunil had to pick to make that number four it had to be the last day of the Headingley Test. Edmonds stepped up to bowl, flighted the ball beautifully and Sunil was gone, comprehensively bowled for 78.

'Never mind', said Sunil, later that night, as the team prepared to move on to Manchester to play Lancashire, 'there's always the last Test.'

That Sunil's 'failure' to score a century for India in the series meant a great deal to him became increasingly obvious in the Oval Test. India batted second, chasing an England total of 305 all out, and Sunil was caught behind for 13, his only negligible score of the summer. Time was running out, the chances were slipping away and Sunil knew that only too well. On the evening of the second day's play we had one of our last chats of a long, eventful summer spent in close contact with each other.

'Hello, Sunil; a pity about today,' I said.

'Ah, the elusive three figures, Chris,' Sunil replied rather sadly. 'Will they never come?'

'There's the second innings yet,' I told him in a feeble attempt to appear hopeful.

'Yes, I'm always optimistic,' Sunil said quietly.

'You know,' I spoke after a pause, 'I hope that I haven't put any pressure on you to score a hundred. I've been talking about it all summer.'

'Oh, no,' Sunil was quick to reassure me. 'No more than 600 million others in India!' He spoke with an infectious laugh and the wistful tinge of sadness with which he began the conversation had disappeared as rapidly as it had materialised.

We did not have the opportunity to speak until the match had ended. By then everything had changed and the game had climaxed in a most amazing way that placed it high in the list of most remarkable Test Matches. Whereas at Lord's imminent defeat had been turned into a courageous draw, the Fourth Test ended with India just two forceful strokes away from one of the most outstanding victories ever achieved in Test history. That it became even remotely possible was due entirely to one player: Sunil Gavaskar. The story of the match revolved around the last day. Until then, nothing outstanding had taken place, with the exception of another immaculate Boycott century in the England second innings. By that stage England appeared to be coasting to a comfortable victory but the arrival of Sunil at the crease put a different complexion on the game. The innings by Sunil was to be hailed in some quarters (no less eminent a judge than Sir Leonard Hutton was one) as one of the best, if not *the* best, in the history of Test cricket.

There was no hint of the drama ahead as the match began with Brearley winning the toss and sending Boycott and Butcher out to open the innings. India stuck to their task well. Gooch and Willey were the only batsmen allowed past the half-century and shortly before lunch on the second day the England innings ended at 305 all out. The score was no more than reasonable. India could feel well satisfied with proceedings to date but not for the first time in the series their batting lacked spirit. The words of Sunil concerning playing to potential were to be proved true once again: the ability was there, the second innings would prove it exactly as at Lord's, but determination and application were not there until very nearly too late.

After Sunil had made his 13 in the first innings, in similar vein, no other batsman could make any headway against the England attack and when the tenth wicket fell at 202 most commentators thought the home side held a comfortable, winning 103-run lead. With Brearley able to declare his second innings at 334 for 8 wickets the result appeared a foregone conclusion. The deficit India faced was a massive 437 runs. To all intents and purposes the cause was lost. Undaunted, Sunil and Chetan Chauhan took to the crease late on the fourth day and from that moment onwards history was in the making.

Chetan may not yet have scored a century in Test cricket but it is significant that he has put together more century partnerships with Sunil than any other batsman. Another one was in the offing and it was to be their highest yet. The pair not only remained together until close of play on the fourth day but were not parted on the final day until they had taken 213 runs off the English bowlers. Oh that England had an opening pair like them! Sunil was in complete command, batting with a flair and confidence he had previously shown in only brief spells in the series. Now, on the last day of the last Test he was showing all his concentration and grit, in a display of batting, the like of which has rarely been seen.

The long-awaited had materialised almost at the last moment. The summer of 1979 had been tantalising but there would be no stopping Sunil now. Nor too would there be any stopping of the clicking of the scoreboard by Sunil's new partner, Dilip Vengsarkar. He took guard when Chauhan fell for 80 and 153 runs rapidly sprang from the pair. Suddenly the England bowlers were worried. What was originally an impossible target for India was now a very real goal to aim for. Vengsarkar went with the score at 356 for 2 wickets, less than 100 runs from the most sensational Test victory of all time but it was at this stage that India, through Venkataraghavan, gave the game back to England. Sunil was still batting like a man possessed, a double century imminent, but his third-wicket partner was the strange choice of Kapil Dev and not Vishwanath the customary number four. It was this tactical switch (and sadly, blunder) that lost India's winning position.

The theory behind Venkataraghavan's promotion of Kapil Dev was simple. Kapil could hit fast and furiously and India needed quick runs to win. Conversely, the Oval is a very large ground and, while Kapil may easily have struck a few sixes on a smaller field, he was unlikely to do so on the wide-open spaces of the Surrey headquarters. Venkataraghavan had made an error that Brearley did not miss. The fielders were spread far and wide and in no time at all Kapil hit up a catch to throw away the initiative India had held all day. Ironically, when Vishwanath did go to the crease he immediately stroked an exquisite cover-drive all along the ground to the boundary. If he had retained his normal place who knows how the story would have ended?

The victory was not to be. Sunil was dismissed for 221, Vishwanath was given out caught by Brearley from a possible bump ball and at close of play India stood at 429 for 8 wickets: 429 against 437. It was as close as that, just 8 runs from a victory made possible almost solely by Sunil. Critics, commentators and public alike were in ecstasy over his performance and, when counting the records that he broke in scoring the double century, there was every reason for appreciating the acclaim he received. They are as follows:

1 221 was Sunil's highest score in Test cricket, beating his previous best of 220 v West Indies.
2 The score was the highest-ever by an Indian player in England, beating Vinoo Mankad's Test score of 184 in 1952.
3 The innings was also the highest by an Indian player in all Tests against England, beating 'Tiger' Pataudi's 203 in 1963–4.
4 He became the first Indian player to score three double hundreds in Tests.
5 On the final day of the Oval Test Sunil scored 179 runs, taking his score from 42 not out to 221. This is an Indian record for the most runs scored in a single day of a Test Match by a player from that country. The previous record, 177 runs in a day, was also held by Sunil.

The timing of the innings was perfect. Sunil had waited until the very last innings of the tour to prove in England that his reputation was fully justified. The doubts of certain critics that he could not perform in England had been dispelled for all time with an innings of magic. It was the ideal way to end a summer that had progressively improved for India with each match. The team could return home with heads held high, despite losing the series by a single game.

There was one sad sequel to a batting display that I had awaited for four months. On the morning of the last day I had walked into the office of a well-known betting firm and enquired what odds were on offer for a Gavaskar century that day.

'Win, lose or draw, that's the only bet you can have,' snapped an old woman behind the counter. After wagering all summer I was too late to scoop the pool on the day Sunil played the innings of a lifetime! And Sunil was much amused when he discovered later what had happened.

Averages for 1979 series v England, 4 Tests, played 4

Tests	Inns	NO	Runs	HS	Average	Bowling:
4	7	0	542	221	77·42	Fielding: 3 ct

Results: England 1, India 0, 3 Tests drawn

Accumulative Record

Tests	Inns	NO	Runs	HS	Average	Bowling: 37–1–116–1
50	93	7	4,947	221	57·52	Fielding: 43 ct

It is fitting to end this book with Sunil Gavaskar's finest hour in Test cricket. A few days later, after the Oval Test, Sunil was once again in action against Australia in India, with more games to follow against Pakistan, also at home. He was restored to the captaincy for those series and the author was in India for part of them but the story of that must wait until another day.

The story ends but not the career. Where that will end, and with how many records to his name, is impossible to tell. What can be said, with conviction, is that Sunil Manohar Gavaskar is a man unique in world cricket today.

APPENDIX

Sunil Gavaskar in Test and First-Class Cricket
compiled by James Gibb and the author

Test Appearances

Year	Opponents	Tests	Venue	Result
1971	West Indies	4	Abroad	India 1 − 0 (4 drawn)
1971	England	3	Abroad	India 1 − 0 (2 drawn)
1972 − 3	England	5	Home	India 2 − 1 (2 drawn)
1974	England	3	Abroad	England 3 − 0
1974 − 5	West Indies	2	Home	West Indies 3 − 2
1976	New Zealand	3	Abroad	Drawn series (1 drawn)
1976	West Indies	4	Abroad	West Indies 2 − 1 (1 drawn)
1976	New Zealand	3	Home	India 2 − 0 (1 drawn)
1976 − 7	England	5	Home	England 3 − 1 (1 drawn)
1977 − 8	Australia	5	Abroad	Australia 3 − 2
1978	Pakistan	3	Abroad	Pakistan 2 − 0 (1 drawn)
1978 − 9	West Indies	6	Home	India 1 − 0 (5 drawn)
1979	England	4	Abroad	England 1 − 0 (3 drawn)
1979	Australia	6	Home	India 2 − 0 (4 drawn)
1979 − 80	Pakistan	6	Home	India 2 − 0 (4 drawn)
1980	England (Jubilee Test)	1	Home	England won

Appearances against Each Country

England	21		Home appearances	34
West Indies	16		Overseas appearances	29
Australia	11			63
Pakistan	9			
New Zealand	6			
	63			

Test-Match Centuries

1	116	v	West Indies	at	Georgetown	March	1971	3rd Test
2	117*	v	West Indies	at	Bridgetown	April	1971	4th Test
3	{124	v	West Indies	at	Port of Spain	April	1971	5th Test }
4	{220	v	West Indies	at	Port of Spain	April	1971	5th Test }
5	101	v	England	at	Old Trafford	June	1974	1st Test
6	116	v	New Zealand	at	Auckland	January	1976	2nd Test
7	156	v	West Indies	at	Port of Spain	March	1976	2nd Test
8	102	v	West Indies	at	Port of Spain	April	1976	3rd Test
9	119	v	New Zealand	at	Bombay	November	1976	1st Test
10	108	v	England	at	Bombay	February	1976	5th Test
11	113	v	Australia	at	Brisbane	December	1977	1st Test
12	127	v	Australia	at	Perth	December	1977	2nd Test
13	118	v	Australia	at	Melbourne	January	1978	3rd Test
14	{111	v	Pakistan	at	Karachi	November	1978	3rd Test }
15	{137	v	Pakistan	at	Karachi	November	1978	3rd Test }
16	205	v	West Indies	at	Bombay	December	1978	1st Test
17	{107	v	West Indies	at	Calcutta	December	1978	3rd Test }
18	{182*	v	West Indies	at	Calcutta	January	1979	3rd Test }
19	120	v	West Indies	at	New Delhi	January	1979	5th Test
20	221	v	England	at	The Oval	September	1979	4th Test
21	115	v	Australia	at	New Delhi	October	1979	4th Test
22	123	v	Australia	at	Bombay	November	1979	6th Test
23	166	v	Pakistan	at	Calcutta	January	1980	5th Test

Double Centuries

				6s	4s	Mins
220	v	West Indies	1970 – 1	—	22	505
205	v	West Indies	1978 – 9	2	27	390
221	v	England	1979	—	21	490

Centuries in Indian Domestic Competitions

1	114	Bombay	v	Rajasthan	April	1970	at	Bombay	Ranji Trophy
2	104	Bombay	v	Gujarat	November	1970	at	Bombay	Ranji Trophy
3	176	Bombay	v	Maharashtra	November	1970	at	Poona	Ranji Trophy
4	101	West Zone	v	East Zone	February	1972	at	Jamshedpur	Duleep Trophy
5	282	Bombay	v	Bihar	March	1972	at	Bombay	Ranji Trophy
6	157	Bombay	v	Bengal	April	1972	at	Bombay	Ranji Trophy
7	160	Bombay	v	Gujarat	January	1973	at	Bombay	Ranji Trophy
8	135	Bombay	v	Madhya Pradesh	March	1973	at	Indore	Ranji Trophy
9	134	Bombay	v	Hyderabad	April	1973	at	Bombay	Ranji Trophy
10	105	Bombay	v	Rest of India	November	1973	at	Bombay	Irani Cup
11	156*	Rest of India	v	Karnataka	October	1974	at	Bangalore	Irani Cup
12	112	Bombay	v	Gujarat	October	1975	at	Ahmedabad	Ranji Trophy
13	190	Bombay	v	Maharashtra	November	1975	at	Bulsar	Ranji Trophy
14	171	Bombay	v	Saurashtra	December	1975	at	Bombay	Ranji Trophy
15	228	West Zone	v	South Zone	October	1976	at	Bombay	Duleep Trophy
16	120	Bombay	v	Tamil Nadu	March	1977	at	Baroda	Ranji Trophy
17	169	West Zone	v	Central Zone	September	1977	at	Bombay	Duleep Trophy
18	105	Bombay	v	Maharashtra	December	1978	at	Ahmedabad	Ranji Trophy
19	204	Bombay	v	Bihar	March	1979	at	Bombay	Ranji Trophy
20	130*	West Zone	v	North Zone	March	1979	at	Bombay	Duleep Trophy

NOTE: Baroda, Gujarat, Maharashtra and Saurashtra comprise the West Zone league of the Ranji Trophy with Bombay.

Totals

Ranji Trophy	14
Duleep Trophy	4
Irani Cup	2

Century Partnerships in Test Cricket

#							
1	112 – 3rd	Gavaskar	(116)	& G. R. Vishwanath (55)	v WI	Georgetown	1970 – 1
2	123 – 1st	Gavaskar	(64)*	& A. V. Mankad (53)*	v WI	Georgetown	1970 – 1
3	122 – 3rd	Gavaskar	(124)	& D. N. Sardesai (75)	v WI	Port of Spain	1970 – 1
4	148 – 2nd	Gavaskar	(220)	& A. L. Wadekar (54)	v WI	Port of Spain	1970 – 1
5	135 – 1st	Gavaskar	(67)	& F. M. Engineer (66)	v Eng	Bombay	1972 – 3
6	131 – 1st	Gavaskar	(49)	& F. M. Engineer (86)	v Eng	Lords	1974
7	168 – 2nd	Gavaskar	(86)	& E. D. Solkar (102)	v WI	Bombay	1974 – 5
8	204 – 2nd	Gavaskar	(116)	& S. Amanath (124)	v NZ	Auckland	1975 – 6
9	204 – 5th	Gavaskar	(156)	& B. P. Patel (115)*	v WI	Port of Spain	1975 – 6
10	108 – 2nd	Gavaskar	(102)	& M. Amanath (85)	v WI	Port of Spain	1975 – 6
11	136 – 1st	Gavaskar	(66)	& A. D. Gaekwad (81)*	v WI	Kingston	1975 – 6
12	120 – 1st	Gavaskar	(119)	& A. D. Gaekwad (42)	v NZ	Bombay	1976 – 7
13	114 – 2nd	Gavaskar	(66)	& M. Amanath (70)	v NZ	Kanpur	1976 – 7
14	139 – 4th	Gavaskar	(108)	& B. P. Patel (83)	v NZ	Bombay	1976 – 7
15	193 – 2nd	Gavaskar	(127)	& M. Amanath (100)	v Aus	Perth	1977 – 8
16	101 – 3rd	Gavaskar	(89)	& G. R. Vishwanath (145)*	v Pak	Faisalabad	1978 – 9
17	192 – 1st	Gavaskar	(97)	& C. P. S. Chauhan (93)	v Pak	Lahore	1978 – 9
18	117 – 2nd	Gavaskar	(137)	& M. Amanath (53)	v Pak	Karachi	1978 – 9
19	155 – 2nd	Gavaskar	(205)	& G. R. Vishwanath (52)	v WI	Bombay	1978 – 9
20	117 – 4th	Gavaskar	(205)	& C. P. S. Chauhan (52)	v WI	Bombay	1978 – 9
21	153 – 1st	Gavaskar	(73)	& C. P. S. Chauhan (84)	v WI	Calcutta	1978 – 9
22	344 – 2nd	Gavaskar	(182)*	& D. B. Vengsarkar (157)*	v WI	Bombay	1978 – 9
23	119 – 1st	Gavaskar	(120)	& C. P. S. Chauhan (60)	v WI	New Delhi	1978 – 9
24	151 – 2nd	Gavaskar	(120)	& D. B. Vengsarkar (109)	v WI	New Delhi	1978 – 9
25	124 – 1st	Gavaskar	(68)	& C. P. S. Chauhan (56)	v Eng	Edgbaston	1979
26	213 – 1st	Gavaskar	(221)	& C. P. S. Chauhan (80)	v Eng	Oval	1979
27	153 – 2nd	Gavaskar	(221)	& D. B. Vengsarkar (52)	v Eng	Oval	1979

28	114 – 1st	Gavaskar	(76)	& C. P. S. Chauhan (58)	v Aus	Kanpur	1979 – 80
29	159 – 3rd	Gavaskar	(115)	& G. R. Vishwanath (131)	v Aus	New Delhi	1979 – 80
30	192 – 1st	Gavaskar	(123)	& C. P. S. Chauhan (73)	v Aus	Bombay	1979 – 80
31	105 – 2nd	Gavaskar	(88)	& D. B. Vengsarkar (33)	v Pak	Bangalore	1979 – 80
32	125 – 1st	Gavaskar	(81)	& C. P. S. Chauhan (61)	v Pak	Kanpur	1979 – 80
33	105 – 5th	Gavaskar	(166)	& Y. P. Sharma (46)	v Pak	Calcutta	1980

Gavaskar's most prolific partner has been C. P. S. Chauhan with whom he has shared 9 three-figure partnerships, only one of which was not made as an opening pair.

Gavaskar has taken part in a record 33 century partnerships for India as follows:

1st	2nd	3rd	4th	5th	6th	7th	8th	9th	10th	Highest
13	12	4	2	2	—	—	—	—	—	344*

Centuries in Representative Matches

1	125	Indians v Trinidad	March	1971	at Pointe-a-Pierre
2	165	Indians v Leicestershire	July	1971	at Leicester
3	194	Indians v Worcestershire	September	1971	at Worcester
4	128	Indians v T. N. Pearce's XI	September	1971	at Scarborough
5	104	Indians v Sri Lanka President's XI	January	1974	at Colombo
6	136	Indians v Surrey	May	1974	at The Oval
7	104*	Indians v Lancashire	May	1974	at Old Trafford
8	203	Indians v Sri Lanka	November	1975	at Hyderabad
9	165*	Indians v Pakistan Banks XI	September	1978	at Karachi
10	166	Indians v Hampshire	July	1979	at Southampton
11	116	Indians v Gloucestershire	July	1979	at Bristol

NOTE: The centuries against Sri Lanka were in matches decreed first class in accordance with ICC rules.

Test Match Aggregates

In All Tests:

Tests	Inns	NO	Runs	HS	Average	100s	50s	Catches
63	114	8	5,974	221	56·35	23	25	52

Against Each Country

	M	L	NO	Runs	HS	Average	100s	50s	Catches
v West Indies	16	28	4	2,004	220	83·50	10	6	8
v England	21	41	1	1,594	221	39·85	3	11	18
v Australia	11	17	0	875	127	51·47	5	2	11
v New Zealand	6	11	1	525	119	52·50	2	2	8
v Pakistan	9	17	2	976	166	65·06	3	4	7
Total	63	114	8	5,951	221	56·14	23	25	52

NOTE: Gavaskar's aggregates against England and West Indies are the highest for India against these countries.

Bowling in Test Cricket

	O	M	Runs	W	Average	Best
v West Indies	1	0	9	0	—	
v England	25	8	56	0	—	
v Australia	6	1	17	0	—	
v New Zealand	—	—	—	—	—	
v Pakistan	10	1	52	1	52·00	1 – 34
Totals	42	10	126	1	126·00	1 – 34

Batting Record

				Opening partner	Opening stand
1970 – 1	c Lloyd b Noreiga	65		A. V. Mankad	68
	not out	67	TSI	A. V. Mankad	74
	c Carew b Sobers	116	TSI TSM	A. V. Mankad	72
	not out	64	TSI	A. V. Mankad	123
	c Holder b Dowe	1		A. V. Mankad	2
	not out	117	TSI	A. V. Mankad	35
	c Lewis b Holford	124	TSI	S. Abid Ali	26
	b Shepherd	220	TSI	S. Abid Ali	11
1971	c Amiss b Price	4		A. V. Mankad	1
	c Edrich b Gifford	53	TSI	A. V. Mankad	8
	c Knott b Price	57	TSI TSM	A. V. Mankad	19
	c Knott b Hutton	24	TSI	A. V. Mankad	9
	b Snow	6		A. V. Mankad	17
	lbw b Snow	0		A. V. Mankad	2
1972 – 3	c Grieg b Arnold	12		R. D. Parkar	17
	c Grieg b Underwood	8		R. D. Parkar	26
	c Old b Underwood	18		R. D. Parkar	29
	lbw b Old	2		R. D. Parkar	2
	c Grieg b Gifford	20		C. P. Chauhan	4
	not out —	0	at no 8	—	
	c Grieg b Birkenshaw	69		C. P. Chauhan	85
	c sub (Wood) b Underwood	24		C. P. Chauhan	8
	b Old	4		F. M. Engineer	25
	c & b Underwood	67	TSI	F. M. Engineer	135
1974	run out	101	TSI TSM	E. D. Solkar	22
	c Hendrick b Old	58	TSI	E. D. Solkar	32
	c Knott b Old	49		F. M. Engineer	131
	lbw b Arnold	5		F. M. Engineer	2
	c Knott b Arnold	0	out first ball	S. S. Naik	0
	c Knott b Old	4		S. S. Naik	6
1974 – 5	c Richards b Holder	14		F. M. Engineer	23
	c Murray b Boyce	0		H. S. Kanitkar	5
	b Gibbs	86		F. M. Engineer	0
	c Fredericks b Roberts	8		F. M. Engineer	2

				Opening partner	Opening stand
1975 – 6	c Turner b Howarth	116⎱		D. B. Vengsarkar	16
	not out	35⎰	TSI	D. B. Vengsarkar	38
	c Burgess b Collinge	22⎱		D. B. Vengsarkar	32
	c Howarth b D. R. Hadlee	71⎰		D. B. Vengsarkar	60
	c Wadsworth b R. J. Hadlee	22		D. B. Vengsarkar	40
	absent hurt	—		—	—
1975 – 6	lbw b Roberts	37⎱		P. Sharma	51
	c Jumadeen b Roberts	1⎰		P. Sharma	4
	c Murray b Holding	156	TSI TSM	D. B. Vengsarkar	1
	lbw b Holding	26⎱		A. D. Gaekwad	22
	c Murray b Jumadeen	102⎰		A. D. Gaekwad	69
	b Holding	66⎱		A. D. Gaekwad	136
	c Julien b Holding	2⎰		D. B. Vengsarkar	5
1976 – 7	c Cairns b Petherick	119⎱	TSI TSM	A. D. Gaekwad	120
	c Burgess b R. J. Hadlee	14⎰		M. Amanath	24
	b O'Sullivan	66⎱		A. D. Gaekwad	79
	b R. J. Hadlee	15⎰		A. D. Gaekwad	23
	b Cairns	2⎱		A. D. Gaekwad	0
	st Lees b O'Sullivan	43⎰		A. D. Gaekwad	33
1976 – 7	c Willis b Lever	38⎱		A. D. Gaekwad	43
	c Woolmer b Underwood	71⎰	TSI TSM	A. D. Gaekwad	20
	c Old b Willis	0⎱		A. D. Gaekwad	1
	b Underwood	18⎰		A. D. Gaekwad	31
	c Brearley b Old	39⎱		M. Amanath	5
	c Woolmer b Underwood	24⎰	TSI	D. B. Vengsarkar (retired hurt)	40
	c Underwood b Lever	4⎱		A. D. Gaekwad	9
	c Brearley b Underwood	50⎰		A. D. Gaekwad	31
	c & b Underwood	108⎱	TSI TSM	A. D. Gaekwad	52
	c Willis b Underwood	42⎰		A. D. Gaekwad	68
1977 – 8	c Cosier b Clark	3⎱		D. B. Vengsarkar	11
	c Rixon b Clark	113⎰	TSI TSM	D. B. Vengsarkar	7
	c Rixon b Clark	4⎱		C. P. Chauhan	14
	b Clark	127⎰	TSI TSM	C. P. Chauhan	47
	c Rixon b Thomson	0⎱		C. P. Chauhan	0
	c Serjeant b Gannon	118⎰	TSI TSM	C. P. Chauhan	40
	c Rixon b Thomson	49		C. P. Chauhan	97

182

Year	Dismissal	Score		Partner	
	c Toohey b Thomson	7		C. P. Chauhan	23
	c Rixon b Callen	29		C. P. Chauhan	40
1978 – 9	b Qasim	89		C. P. Chauhan	97
	not out	8		C. P. Chauhan	43
	c Majid b Salim	5		C. P. Chauhan	15
	c Sarfraz b Mushtag	97	TSI TSM	C. P. Chauhan	192
	c Sarfraz b Imran	111	TSI	C. P. Chauhan	58
	c Wasim Bari b Sarfraz	137	TSI TSM	C. P. Chauhan	5
1978 – 9	b Clarke	205	TSI TSM	C. P. Chauhan	35
	c Murray b Clarke	73		C. P. Chauhan	153
	c Shivnarine b Clarke	0	out first ball	A. D. Gaekwad	0
	c Bacchus b Phillip	107	TSI	C. P. Chauhan	20
	not out	182	TSI TSM	A. D. Gaekwad	17
	c Bacchus b Phillip	4		C. P. Chauhan	10
	c Murray b Clarke	1		C. P. Chauhan	16
	c Murray b Clarke	120		C. P. Chauhan	119
	c Murray b Marshall	40		C. P. Chauhan	51
1979	run out	61		C. P. Chauhan	15
	c Gooch b Hendrick	68	TSI	C. P. Chauhan	124
	c Taylor b Gooch	42	TSI	C. P. Chauhan	12
	c Brearley b Botham	59		C. P. Chauhan	79
	b Edmonds	78	TSI TSM	C. P. Chauhan	1
	c Bairstow b Botham	13		C. P. Chauhan	9
	c Gower b Botham	221	TSI TSM	C. P. Chauhan	213
1979 – 80	c Wood b Hogg	50		C. P. Chauhan	80
	c Hilditch b Yardley	10		C. P. Chauhan	22
	lbw b Dymock	76	TSI	C. P. Chauhan	114
	c Whatmore b Yardley	12		C. P. Chauhan	24
	lbw b Higgs	115		C. P. Chauhan	38
	lbw b Hogg	14		C. P. Chauhan	15
	c Hilditch b Dymock	25		C. P. Chauhan	52
	c Hughes b Border	123	TSI TSM	C. P. Chauhan	192
	c Miandad b Qadir	88	TSI TSM	C. P. Chauhan	17
	c Bari b Sikander	31	TSI	C. P. Chauhan	19
	c Bari b Sikander	21		C. P. Chauhan	37
	c Qadir b Sikander	4		C. P. Chauhan	

				Opening partner	Opening stand
	c Zaheer b Qasim	48	TSI	C. P. Chauhan	
	b Qasim	2		C. P. Chauhan	
	c Majid b Ehtashamuddin	81	TSI TSM	C. P. Chauhan	125
	c Qasim b Imran	166	TSI TSM	C. P. Chauhan	
	not out	29		C. P. Chauhan	
	c Qasim b Imran	44		C. P. Chauhan	
	c Miandad b Imran	15		C. P. Chauhan	
1980	c Taylor b Botham	49	TSI	R. Binny	
	c Taylor b Botham	24		R. Binny	

NOTES: TSI = Top Score in Innings (39 times); TSM = Top Score in Match for India (21 times).

184

Mode of Dismissal

Bowled	LBW	Ct		Run Out	Stumped	No	Total
14	8	81 (26 by wktkr)		2	1	8	114

Bowlers who have dismissed Gavaskar most times

D. L. Underwood	10
C. M. Old	6
I. T. Botham	5
S. T. Clarke	5
Sikander Bakht	4
W. M. Clark	4
Imran Khan	4
M. A. Holding	4

Opening Partners in Tests

		Best	100
C. P. S. Chauhan	49	213	8
A. D. Gaekwad	18	136	2
A. V. Mankad	12	123*	1
F. M. Engineer	7	135	2
D. B. Vengsarkar	10	60	
R. D. Parkar	4	29	
S. Abid Ali	2	26	
E. D. Solkar	2	32	
S. S. Naik	2	6	
P. Sharma	2	51	
M. Amanath	2	24	
R. Binny	2		
H. S. Kantikar	1	5	
	99		

NOTE: Gavaskar batted at 8 because of injury in the second innings v England at Madras in 1972 – 3, in the only occasion on which he had not opened the batting in Tests.

Records in Indian Test Cricket

For India

1 Most runs in Tests, 5,951, average 56.14. Next highest is currently G. R. Vishwanath.

2 Most runs in Test series, 774, average 154·80, v West Indies in 1970–1. Gavaskar is the only Indian to score 700 runs in a Test series and has now done this twice.

3 Most centuries in Tests, 23 in 63 matches. Previous highest for India was 12, by P. R. Umrigar. (G. R. Vishwanath currently has 11 centuries). Gavaskar's average of one century every 4·59 innings has only been exceeded in all Test cricket by D. G. Bradman (2·75) and G. A. Headley (4·00).

4 Most centuries in one Test series: 4 v West Indies in 1970–1 and again in 1978–9.

5 Most half-centuries for India: 25, G. R. Vishwanath is currently next with 20.

6 Gavaskar is the only Indian to score a Test century in six different countries. He achieved this feat when he made 111 v Pakistan at Karachi in 1978–9.

7 Gavaskar is also the only Indian batsman to score three Test centuries in consecutive innings on two occasions. In 1970–1 he made 117*, 124 and 220 v West Indies, and in 1978–9 he scored 111 and 137 v Pakistan then 205 v West Indies.

8 Gavaskar holds Indian records for the highest innings v England (221 at the Oval in 1979, beating the Nawab of Pataudi's 203* at New Delhi in 1963–4) and v West Indies (220 at Port of Spain in 1970–1, beating D. N. Sardesai's 212 at Bridgetown in the same series).

9 Gavaskar holds the Indian record for the most runs scored by a batsman in a day in a Test match: 179, going from 42* to 221 on the last day of the Fourth Test v England at the Oval in 1979. The previous record, 177, was also held by Gavaskar.

10 Gavaskar is the only Indian player to score a century and a double century in the same Test, v West Indies at Port of Spain in 1970–1.

11 Currently Gavaskar has the highest batting average (56.14) by any player appearing for India.

12 Gavaskar established a unique record at Bombay's Wankhede Stadium when he scored centuries there in four consecutive Test matches between 1976 and 1979. His scores were 119 v New Zealand, 1976; 108 v England, 1977; 205 v West Indies,

1978; and 123 v Australia, 1979. Gavaskar also holds the same record at Port of Spain, Trinidad, where he scored four centuries in three consecutive Tests against West Indies: 124 and 220 in the Fifth Test, 1971, and 156 and 102 in the Second and Third Tests of the 1976 series.

World Test Records

1 Most centuries by a regular opening batsman in Test cricket (23). Sir Leonard Hutton held the previous record for an opener with 19.
2 Most runs in a debut series: 774 in only four Tests v West Indies in 1970–1 for a remarkable average of 154·80. Previously the highest in a first series was 703 runs (average 87·87) by George Headley of West Indies in 1929–30.
3 Gavaskar is the only man to score two separate centuries. in a Test match on three occasions. Four players have done this twice, Herbert Sutcliffe, George Headley, Clyde Walcott and Greg Chappell.
4 Most runs by any player in a 12-month period in Test cricket: 1,984 runs in 17 Tests and 27 innings between 17 October 1978 and 13 October 1979 (average 79·36). The previous record was 1,811 runs by Vivian Richards of West Indies between 28 November 1975 and 13 August 1976 (14 Tests, 24 innings, average 75·45).
5 Gavaskar is the only man to score 1,000 Test runs in a Calendar year three times: 1,024 in 1976, 1,044 in 1978 and 1,721 in 1979. Only Ken Barrington has achieved this feat twice.

Index